LEAVING NEW ORLEANS

An Unsettling Tale

To Cheryl who found me a home. Sally

Sally Cole

To Chris, Davy, and Kate,
To the people of New Orleans,
And to those not from New Orleans, who took us in.

Acknowledgements

Thank you to all the family members and friends who read my manuscript and cheered me on: Wendy Cole and Lacey Singleton, two of my earliest readers; Kate, Davy, and Chris Mooney; Tom Cole, Catherine Loomis, Del McGinnis, Daf Rutz, Laure Kagan, Anthea Bruffee, Don Bruce, Frank Crothers, and Nancy Richard. Special thanks to Jessica Munns, who organized a Katrina conference at the University of Denver and invited me to read, and to Cynthia Hogue, poet par excellence, whose kind words encouraged me. I am grateful to the students whose writing samples enhanced my story and to my brother Tom for his technical expertise in preparing the manuscript. Finally, my deepest thanks to those who gave me shelter from the storm —Don Bruce, Elena Saxonhouse, and her roommates — and to the residents of Baderville, who helped me in more ways than I can name.

Whoever said, "Winter's not a season; it's an occupation," must have lived in Baderville. In the morning, the house at 56 degrees, I want a fire, fast. But nothing comes easy here. First, I must clean the wood stove, every morning deep in ash, a residue, I've learned, that will choke the fire and settle over furniture every time I open the door to poke the embers or add another log. And then there's the arsenic in the ashes, my soil-scientist neighbor tells me, that I should try not to inhale. But how not to? All I want is ready heat, but first I venture out into the cold, as much as twelve below zero, to retrieve my ash pail from its spot in the snow. Inside, I shovel my ashes into the pail, inevitably spilling on the hearth, then take it outside, away from the house, making sure to clamp on the lid.

It's my first winter here, seven miles outside Flagstaff, in a house at the end of a quarter-mile cinder road, now socked in with knee-deep snow, behind me the national forest where, at 7300 feet, elk roam and by law no one can ever build. But even I, a rookie, know the danger of those ashes that feel cold to the touch but harbor deep inside an ember or two that, smoldering beneath the surface, can set fire to deck or house or tree. In December a neighbor burned his house beyond repair when an ember ignited his deck. The newspaper tells us similar tales. So I follow a cautious drill: After twenty-four hours I transfer the ashes from the pail into a hard plastic tub, used once for baby bathing, back when my parents lived here in retirement and we, the children, visited with our broods. At least a day after the tub, I transfer the ashes to a plastic bag, and carry them through the snow to the spot, halfway down my driveway, where I've parked my trash can for the winter. No

February 2008, Baderville

1

one, and certainly not a garbage truck, could make it up my driveway in the winter, and the garbage man refuses, even in the summer, to navigate my road. So I haul, I shovel, and I make a fire, every morning to heat my house to a balmy 65 degrees.

So much labor, just to start the day. And yet, most mornings, I enjoy the rituals, the connection to the weather, the winds, and the sky that living here forces on me. On a clear day, I can factor solar heat into my toil, let my fire die by noon when, by opening blinds I can capture the heat through a bank of south-facing windows, ceiling to floor, that my parents made into a solar room. Even on a February day the sun through those windows can heat the room to 90 degrees. At 3:30 or so, by opening the sunroom door, I can raise the entire house to 68 degrees as the heated air rises up three steps to the house's main level.

And so my labor eases. Living here, I watch the sun, I raise and lower blinds, I live "deliberately," or so I like to think, as Thoreau, this house's inspiration, exhorts us all to do.

May 2007, New Orleans

Eight months ago I had formaldehyde, not arsenic, on my mind. My FEMA trailer, number 30, sat at the edge of Holt Cemetery, a pauper's graveyard, on a plot my employer, Delgado Community College, had set aside for its "family" after Katrina walloped New Orleans on Black Monday: August 29th, 2005. Between the baseball field and the cemetery, faculty and staff, uniformly homeless, moved their meager possessions into these compact, though reeking, homes, throwing open windows to the humid air, and cranking up the AC to counteract that outside steam. Even at night, we all slept with windows open, even though anyone, by merely pushing in the detachable screens, could murder us in our beds. All those years of living in New Orleans, from my first summer in 1979, I had slept with doors locked, windows securely latched, in a town whose daily murder rate often rivaled the body count in Iraq. But now, weighing the evils of formaldehyde against the black hearts of the city's thugs, we opt for clear lungs believing, in the magical way most humans reason, that having lost once, so randomly and undeservedly, we've been granted a reprieve. And so, lying in my bed with its prosaic white sheets and standard-issue pillows, I feel strangely at peace.

In the middle of the night a light rain begins to fall, eliciting a chorus from the frogs who inhabit the stagnant pools amid the gravesites. I could be in a cottage on some country road outside Natchitoches or Lafayette, not in this ruined city, its storm debris still piled on the neutral grounds, its storm-lashed houses still bearing the cryptic graffiti of the National Guard: X, 9/7, 0, signifying date of entry, bodies found. So strange it is to lie here, listening to

a sound I've never heard in all my pungent city nights, a
hard-won, post-storm gift.

Lying in another of the many beds I've slept in since Katrina—for I'll never sleep in my own bed again—I wake to the sound of sirens and remember I'm in DC, an evacuee, with my Red Cross debit card and my strange mish-mash of a wardrobe whose style I've come to think of as "evacuee chic." A strange barking follows the sirens, dog-like, and yet not quite like any dog I've ever heard. I ask Elena, my elder son's girlfriend, who, in an act of kindness, has taken me in. I've become the fourth, though nonpaying, tenant in a three-story house in Woodley Park. "That's the gibbons from the zoo," she tells me. "The sirens from Cheney's motorcade coming down Connecticut Avenue set them off." And so, on weekday mornings for the three weeks I live here, I lie awake, as if in some Sumatran jungle, while the gibbons whoop me into another day.

In my waking hours, I pretend I'm a tourist, living out of a suitcase, and take in the city's sights: the zoo, the National Cathedral, the Vietnam Memorial, the museums, all of which I access by foot, although it takes me hours to walk to the Mall and then back uphill in a climate as steamy as the one I left behind. I have hours to kill and a body to wear out so that, ideally, I can sleep until the sirens sound. But no matter how exhausted I've become, I still awaken in the night, my wall of denial punched through, to confront the truth. I'm not a tourist; I'm a refugee, the label we've all shunned because it hits too close to home. That suitcase contains everything I own in the world: the three days of clothes I brought with me, merged with the kind togs of strangers. I am banished until the mayor lifts the prohibition and calls back the citizens, neighborhood by neighborhood—Broadmoor, Gentilly, New Orleans East, Lakeview—not to resettle, but to "look and leave."

In the meantime, I wander over the bridge to the coffeehouse Tryst; to the restaurant Chipotle, where evacuees are given free food; and often to the zoo, where a newborn panda, too young for our viewing, grows behind the keeper's door. The cub embodies my waiting, that of us all, our hopes. When the mayor calls back Lakeview, the panda cub is still hidden from view, but I can watch him on the internet, wobbly, alive.

Water is wet; fire is hot, or so I thought before I moved to Flagstaff. The intricacies of wood—aspen, juniper, pitch pine, pine—alone and in combination I had yet to discover. But now, as I have slowly learned, fire is hot, or hotter, or white-glowing lava-hot, depending on the wood, the quantity of embers, the chimney's draw. Three months into winter, as I shovel my ashes, I sift the charcoal from the ash, leaving the biggest chunks behind to kick-start my fire, prolong its blaze. I start with pitch pine, a first-string player, that instantly ignites with a flame that wraps around and pulsates, sparking into my second choice, aspen— clean-burning, ash-grey—less flashy than pitch pine but solid and true. Juniper, shaggy-barked and dense, follows, but before I toss it to the flame I inhale deeply. That smell brings back memories—of hamsters, of campfires from my childhood. Juniper, my Madeleine.

Drinking my coffee before the stove, I turn the wood, I poke the embers, I add a log, I watch the pan of water that I keep on the stovetop to humidify the house and to signal the moment when I dare to call in the second-string: pine, ubiquitous pine, which I have in abundance, thanks to my neighbors, who thinned the woods behind their house (technically my land) to protect their property from the summer's fires. They chopped and stacked the wood, then gave it to me. When the water in the pan boils, or even better comes to a rolling boil, I add a pine log with no fear of harm. But one more will cool the fire, bring the boil to simmer, as a single player can slow down the game, a bass player drag, throwing off the tempo. Sometimes for hours I orchestrate my fire. Although I'm retired, it's an occupation. And yet I draw my line. I refuse to extend my watch into

7

the night, as many others do, waking at all hours to stoke their fires. I'd rather wake to a frigid house, my bed, with its flannel sheets, its comforter, keeping me warm.

The fire dies; I bring it back to life; I embolden my pine by removing its bark, using as a lever my FEMA-issued knife, cheap and expendable, a link to my past—like my Red Cross debit card, which I used to scrape the first snowfall from my windshield, or my extra care with fire and ash, Katrina's legacy: my fear of losing it all again.

One afternoon, from my open window, I hear a new sound over the hum of my air conditioner and the periodic clink of baseballs connecting with metal bats on the northern edge of the trailer park. A black man is digging a grave not ten yards from my open window. The next afternoon the mourners arrive, a dozen women, men and children, in their finest clothes—not black, but blue and even red. The hearse unloads a high-end casket, its case belying the indignity of its resting place. I close my window, feeling I'm intruding on a private scene. I can only imagine the words being said, the hymns sung, the relationship of mourners to deceased, the story behind this undignified end. But it's over in minutes. The mourners leave, the hearse retreats, the same lone black man fills in the open pit. That night I think of my quiet new neighbor, imagine a mist rising over his grave.

In the morning I carry my coffee into the graveyard to pay him a visit: I find nothing but a lumpy mound—no flowers, no headstone, not even a trace of the life here extinguished. At other sites, more effort has been made, touching tributes penned in Sharpie on concrete blocks, plastic flowers placed on graves, sometimes a makeshift fence protecting a loved one from the chaos around him: broken headstones, muddy puddles, shattered glass, mere remnants of grass. The only beauty rises in the limbs of an occasional oak tree hung with Spanish moss.

Near the southern boundary of the cemetery, facing Bud's Broiler on City Park Avenue, stands a monument to Buddy Bolden, buried here somewhere in an unmarked plot. "The blowingest man since Gabriel," the inscription tells us—next to Louis Armstrong, our city's favorite son.

Some jazz aficionado has left a bottle of Kentucky's finest bourbon at the foot of the monument, an inch of liquid still remaining. I try to picture the tributes paid here after dark: a trumpet blast, a toast, a ritualistic passing of the whiskey vial. Weeks later, on a Sunday morning, I will find scattered here, around the now near-empty bottle, a dozen quarters. It's laundry day, when I will join a handful of Latino workers at a laundromat on Maple Street. I could use those quarters. But deep within my rationalist soul lies a strange fear of gris-gris. I leave the money there.

Two weeks before I pack up my trailer and relocate to Flagstaff, I witness my final burial. The lone black man prepares the gravesite; the following morning the mourners come. An even more ostentatious casket is lifted from the hearse. A similarly well-dressed gathering of African-Americans mourn. Again, I close my windows and busy myself in my kitchen. When I next look out, all but two of the mourners and the hearse are gone. The two remaining—young black men—stand in the shade of a large oak tree. The casket sits atop the grave, too large for the opening, as the gravedigger shovels around the perimeter until he and the mourners can lower the casket into the hole. Before the three leave, they toss the floral arrangement from the casket unceremoniously onto the grave.

For days I relive this scene, reexperience the mourners' shame. As a ceremony veers from its scripted path, a life has somehow careened off course. When I wander one last time through Holt Cemetery, saying goodbye, the flowers on the grave are wilted and brown. By the time winter comes to Flagstaff, there will be no sign that anyone lies buried here.

Before the storm, back when calendars bore with confidence an inked-in future, I had envisioned marching on Washington, on September 24, 2005, in a massive protest of the war in Iraq. Then the realities of work and money killed that dream. I remember thinking at the time how sad it would be if I went to my grave having never marched through the Capital's streets, chanting, placard held high. Now, in a strange twist of fate, I find myself in Woodley Park on that very day.

I set out early, in my new Payless sneakers (bought with my dwindling Red Cross funds) and my patchwork wardrobe—one part purchased, three parts charity—the very picture of the sign I envision but never actually carry: "Katrina Evacuee for Peace." I stop at an ATM across Connecticut from my older son's apartment. He and some friends are sitting outside a coffee house, enjoying the Saturday sun.

"I'm marching on Washington," I announce.

"You can't march *on* Washington when you're *in* Washington," my son replies. (Like me, he majored in English).

"Shut up," I tell him. "I'm marching *on* Washington."

And off I go, flashing them a grin. His friends shout out subway advice, but I'm marching all the way—down Connecticut to Dupont Circle, past the Starbucks and Kramer's Books, through Lafayette Square, to 15th Street, and finally to Constitution.

By the time I reach the Mall, a huge crowd jostles me toward the staging area: throngs of gray-haired hippie types, college kids, children, young couples, all buoyed by the deep-set belief that we can alter the course of history. I

11

pass two women, gray-haired, fiftyish, holding up a sign: "Breasts, Not Bombs." True to their word, they are naked from the waist up. I fall in for awhile with a group from New Orleans, walk proudly beneath their retrofitted sign: "Make Levees, Not War," then stop and start behind a death-masked dozen who periodically die in the street before me, then rise up and march on. I pass Vietnam Veterans for Peace, Iraq Veterans for Peace, Hotel Workers for Peace, every imaginable peace-loving group. I marvel at the wit of the signs people carry: "Quagmire Accomplished," "Yee-haw Is Not a Foreign Policy," wish I had made an effort and were holding mine.

The crowd—one-hundred fifty thousand, the newspaper will tell us—grows rowdier as we near the White House. There, street performers add color to the scene. One man, in a startlingly life-like Cheney mask, holds the strings to his marionette: another man in a dead-on mask of President Bush. I watch as the Cheney/master lets out, then reels in his puppet/leader. In a grand finale, he pulls Bush close until they lock in an obscene embrace.

Eventually I fall out, exhausted, and start my long walk back—uphill to the house in Woodley Park, my mind a surreal whirl of remnants from the march: the chanting, the dying, the puppet show, the hanging breasts. The streets, so orderly this morning, lose me in diagonals and roundabouts. The hills are steeper than I recall, the sunshine hotter. On Calvert, just blocks from my destination, the mural of Marilyn Monroe seems to bob like a protest sign. That night I fall into bed so tired that I sleep through the night. When the gibbons wake me in the morning, somehow their whoops don't sound quite so strange.

12

On February 21st I wake to the aftermath of an overnight snowstorm, one of many since the initial event this winter on December 1st. It's the snowiest year one neighbor can recall since she moved here from Tucson in 1975. I have been dubbed an extreme-weather magnet by the Baderville locals, who still see me as a storm evacuee. The trees bow beneath the weight of snow. When I walk down my driveway to retrieve my paper—a half mile round trip before my first cup of coffee—I must duck underneath one hanging branch. My otherwise pristine path has been broken by Edna, my neighbor's Res dog, who loves the snow. I often find her outside the stall of Charlie, the horse I greet every morning as I hike down and back. Outside the houses on Suzette, where my mailbox stands, the morning labors have begun. People shovel snow, feed their horses, plow their driveways, dig out their cars. Across the meadow, the San Francisco Peaks are half-hidden by clouds.

Those peaks, extinct volcanoes, are sacred to thirteen Indian tribes, among them the Navajo, whose name for them translates "Shining on Top," and the Hopi, for whom they are "The Place of Snow at the Very Top." When this three-day storm blows over, revealing those peaks—Agassiz, centered in my picture window; Fremont, off center to my right; and Humphreys, behind to the left (at 12,633 feet, the highest point in Arizona)—those names will ring true. The snowy peaks will shine in the sun, the trees below them dusted like Alpine beignets.

When the snow ends and sun returns, I resume my long walks through the neighborhood, down Suzette, across Bader, to where Rudd Tank ends in a cul-de-sac, and then beyond, into the national forest; or, alternately, down Bader toward Highway 180, left on Mountain Shadows, and into the Experimental Forest, a large stand of ponderosa set aside for a Forest Service study of fire and forest restoration. Each house I pass tilts toward the peaks, its large windows framing their southern face, its deck spilling out for a closer view. So many disparate lives are bound by this constant—horse owners, single moms, retirees, ski freaks—waking to the mountain as they open their blinds, then gazing out, before drawing them at dusk, on that same wedge of stillness.

In the summer and fall, before the snows came, I'd drive up the mountain to look back from its vantage point. Seven miles up the Snowbowl Road, I could park and ride the chair-lift up Agassiz where, from an elevation of 11,000 feet, I could see my house, a brown speck at the edge of the woods, then, turning north, the glow of the Grand Canyon, seventy miles away. Other times, I'd hike on the Kachina Trail, an easy route wrapping around the mountain's face and opening up to views of the town: the train tracks, the Skydome on the campus of NAU. The first time I ventured onto this trail, I stopped, puzzled, a half-hour in as I heard the sound of a brook rushing by, but even with binoculars could find no water. And then it struck me. Looking up, I saw against the sky a quivering of yellow, the leaves in the wind like water over rocks. I was underneath a stand of aspens. I was all alone. And then I felt it, a creeping panic that would overcome me every time I'd attempt to hike, an urbanite, confronting a primordial fear. It would be almost six months before I conquered this demon, made it to the end of a hiking trail. That night, at the Ski Lift Lodge, I would announce to my neighbors: "I hiked the entire Oldham Trail—3.2 miles in and 3.2 miles back—and I didn't panic; I didn't get lost." My audience would stare back blankly, unable to fathom the source of my pride;

longtime hikers, mountain bikers, horseback riders, skiers, unable to imagine losing their way or feeling, even for a moment, afraid.

One evening a few weeks later, just before closing my blinds, I take a final look at the peaks, their outline hyper-sharp in the sun's fading light. From the corner of my eye, I notice a movement: an elk has entered into the clearing just beneath my window where, like me, it seems to gaze at the peaks. The darkness rolls across the meadow, then climbs up the mountain's skirt, higher and higher, over pine and aspen, up the Snowbowl Road. When I lower my blinds, I see the elk bound away. Night comes to Baderville. Above the darkness, the peaks catch the last light, all three shining on top.

In the mornings outside trailer 30, doors slam, high heels wobble over loose-strewn rocks, chain-link gates clink, then cars start up in the parking lot as faculty and staff set off to work. I put on my running clothes and lock up my trailer, carrying my key and two quarters for the paper.

Across Marconi, I start to run along the sidewalks bordering City Park. Turning east on City Park Avenue, I jog under leafy oaks—still majestic—their long limbs dipping low, some even brushing the ground; then over the footbridge past the Dueling Oak—still standing—ancient and knobby, by the south wall of the Art Museum. But turning right, around the museum, I lower my gaze. The ground must dip imperceptibly beneath my feet; the brackish waters must have pooled here, along the promenade that stretches from the statue of General Beauregard down to the reflecting pool outside the museum's steps. Before the storm, from either side of this passageway, live oaks grew in perfect symmetry, a deep green colonnade, meeting overhead. Through a filtered light, obscured by these trees, the museum held a dreamy allure. Now the trees struggle to survive. Some are clearly dead, others poking up like broccoli spears. The light is all wrong. The museum rises gracelessly, its blocky shape laid bare.

It's just as bad along Roosevelt Mall, across a WPA-built bridge, the avenue lined with concrete benches. The trees all ail. I turn into the practice track, built back in 1992 when New Orleans hosted the Olympic Trials, do one lap, then circle back the way I came—past the museum, over the footbridge to the last, best stretch of my run, along that unscathed stand of healthy trees. There, facing Ralph's on the Park, its back to the bayou, sits my favorite statue: a nymph atop an empty fountain. Her head, tilting to the right, mirrors the curve of the oak limbs overhead, both statue and fountain dappled in light.

At the corner of Marconi and City Park Avenue I drop my quarters into a dispenser and pull out a Picayune, then cut through the campus to the trailer park. While I was gone, someone roped off a section of the parking lot. Now tow truck drivers ferry in, one after another, a rusted mangle of totaled cars, which they line up along the fence of the baseball field. Each car flaunts its tragic end, in plain view of the trailer park. In quantity, they overwhelm. I think of the city streets so recently lined with flooded cars, the freeway overpasses sheltering more—50,000 altogether —each one silt-coated, coffin-like. I think of the ruined home each FEMA trailer represents, each resident's pain still palpable.

Tomorrow continues in this same vein, as we learn the reason for the cars. All day, Jaws of Life in hand, students will extricate "drivers" from these wrecks. The afternoon will end with life-like dummies lying in the parking lot, some cars now roofless, doors ripped off and tossed aside, coke cans and other debris littering the asphalt. We know it's a drill, but it's easy to suspend our disbelief, so fresh are we from our own real traumas: entrapments, rescues, narrow escapes.

On the steps to the trailer nearest the gate, stands my neighbor, a witty black man who watches our comings and goings like a FEMA version of a Wal-Mart greeter. I throw out a suggestion: "We need to complain about this." "Not me," he answers. "They might make me start paying rent!" I laugh and head in to my shower. Once before, as I returned from a run, he met me with a question: "How far you walk?" "I run two and a half miles," I answered.

17

"Whoa," was his reply. "You ain't no nice thing!" I laughed again, the syntax foreign but the meaning clear: "hard core." A few nights later, our lot finally cleared of wrecks, a car pulls up to the gate, blowing its horn for a friend to come out. Our greeter/guard emerges from his trailer. "Why you do me this?" he asks. In the car sit two black women. His complaint veers into banter, flirtation. "Why you treat me so bad?" "We're sorry," they laugh. And then, in a mocking plaint, he clinches his case: "You treat me so bad. You treat me like I live here!"

In late May, despite this city's characters, its pockets of beauty, I will no longer live here, will extricate myself from trailer 30, a process of pain, second-guessing, nostalgia, remorse. New Orleans has become itself a kind of formaldehyde, toxic to the spirit. My compact Mazda can hold everything I own. It's time to go.

Months later—snow whirling, the peaks socked in—I revisit New Orleans via internet. Under the overpass at Canal and Claiborne, where flooded cars once awaited tow-trucks, two hundred citizens live in tents. At the art museum, the ruined oaks have been chopped down and carted away. In their place stand crepe myrtles—flame-topped—in parallel rows like dwarfed sentries. If these trees survive two hundred years, through freeze and flood and wilting heat, their limbs will still never meet overhead or soften the museum's contours. They will remain neat, pretty, generic—like those along sidewalks in Dallas.

One week before I marched on Washington, I again had Katrina to thank for driving me out of New Orleans and into DC, this time for the 2005 Thelonious Monk International Jazz Competition. Months before, my son Davy had auditioned by tape and made the cut. Then the storm chased him out of town with only his hopes and his jazz guitar. Now Elena, older brother Chris, Davy's wife Angela, and I wait inside the Smithsonian to watch ten semi-finalists, all under thirty, vie for the top three spots. Davy has been rendered presentable by Jim Tozzi, a Washington consultant featured in Chris's just-published book, *The Republican War on Science*. From his suit, to his belt, down even to his socks, Davy now blends in with the other nine, thanks to the kindness of this man. No one would ever suspect that he had left town in flip flops three weeks ago, not even a pair of sneakers in tow. Somehow he has carved some practice time out of long hours spent calling FEMA and sneaking his dog in and out of the no-pets apartment that Chris has ceded to him and his wife.

Chris and I are giddy with excitement as the first contestant starts to play. Added to our nervousness for Davy—number seven on the program—is a scheduling glitch: this same afternoon Chris has a book talk at Politics and Prose, across town from the Mall. After Davy performs, we'll have to run.

The first few candidates sound much the same. Then the fifth has something that sets him apart. "There's one," we whisper to each other, checking our watches.

Soon Davy takes the stage, cradling the hollow-bodied seven-string guitar that musicians from New Orleans all seem to play. He dips his knees; he closes his eyes; he plays an original tune I've always loved and joked that I inspired. But "Wrinkles" is a tribute not to an aging mom, but to Kurt Rosenwinkle, a jazz guitarist that Davy admires. After "Wrinkles," he slows things down, uses harp harmonics, plays with an emotion Katrina must have helped create. Before the applause ends, we are running for the door, hailing a cab, once inside exclaiming, over and over, "He was fabulous." "He's made it." "I know he's made it." By day's end we will have earned, hands down, the cabby's prize for "Most Annoying Fare." But we can't help it; we're just that high.

The day keeps getting better. The bookstore where Chris will speak is packed, C-Span camera set up in the aisle. The talk inspires a volley of questions, which I hear with one ear, the other tuned to the door behind me, waiting for Davy to arrive. Chris is finished before his brother comes in, the results written plainly on his face: he's a finalist, slated to play again at the Kennedy Center tomorrow night. Watching my two sons interact, I bask in the moment, feeling as I have many times since Katrina, both sated and bereft.

The following evening, Davy comes in third, but being a finalist is enough. Afterwards, we troop upstairs for the post-contest party. The food is sumptuous, the wine flows, as I wander through the crowd in my care-package party dress, at least ten years out of style, and a new pair of Payless sandals. I meet a man who, like me, has fled here from New Orleans, his finalist son long settled in New York. After congratulating each other on our sons' performances, we trade storm stories, discover we've both just lost our homes. I'm floored by the odds: in an international jazz competition, one-third of the finalists' parents have fallen prey to the same named storm. We wish each other luck, unable to imagine now how much we're going to need it, and move on through the crowd.

Across the buffet I see Lando Calrissian, an aged Billy Dee Williams, the program's emcee. Behind him a photographer snaps a picture of Davy and Angela with pianist/judge Herbie Hancock. Not far off, chatting in a small group, stands Thelonious Monk, Jr., with his bald head and stylish clothes the very essence of jazz-cat hip. Near him, alone, is a man that looks familiar. It's Pat Martino—whose face I know from the instructional tapes I bought for Davy years ago—tonight a Monk competition judge. He's as small as I am, his shoulders even narrower, but the grip of his handshake leaves no doubt: he's a man who makes his living playing the guitar. He exudes calm—has the warmth of a big, barrel-chested man. I tell him how I knew his face; he praises Davy and then adds: "After what he's been through, it's a wonder he could even string his guitar."

The next day, the party like a teasing dream, I'm back to my daily drill: call FEMA, call Delgado, call Farmers, call Fidelity, wander the city, daydream, despair. The computer now confirms what we gleaned from TV weeks ago, water lapping at gutter tops, voiceovers calling out the losers' names—Ninth Ward, St. Bernard, and always Lakeview. But this program isolates single homes, with data leaving no room for doubt. I plug in 6229 Memphis and watch the numbers rise on the screen: 9.9, marking feet of water in my street. On a whim, I punch in my ex-husband's street address—0.0—a further proof that there is no God. My daughter Kate, away at college, has learned of this website and emails me, her message so brief and eloquent I wish I'd saved it for her children: "Mom! I can't believe we're fucking homeless!" Only Davy remains in limbo, neither winner nor loser, his street earning a 4.1, like some diver who forgot to point his toes.

Roaming the streets that afternoon, I try to call up the night before—the gleam of Davy's seven-string, the buttery notes, the camera's flash—but it fades before the certitude of 9.9. A crowd flows down 18th Street, the odor of Thai food in the air. Outside Tryst, a man asks me for directions. "I'm from New Orleans," I answer. "I'm lost myself.

It's quiet in Baderville, the elk gone south, the deep-piled snow like acoustic tiles, keeping us silent and white. In the middle of the night I wake to stillness, light pouring in through my white cotton drapes. It's three a. m. Out the upstairs window I scan the sky, see the moon like a spotlight over the forest, a single star beneath it, low to the west. The snow looks different than it does in the day—whiter—but an eggshell white, a white without sheen, a dead-white white. The trees cast shadows—moon shadows—almost black against the snow. There's not a sound, not a quiver of breeze, not an animal cry. I remember the song by Cat Stevens, or at least its refrain: "I'm being followed by a moon shadow, moon shadow, moon shadow." But I don't remember ever seeing shadows like these, cast by this light.

[About now, in New Orleans, the street lights will be buzzing with static, blurred halos forming around them in the humid air. The bars will still be open, teenagers without curfews drunk-driving home. On Frenchmen Street the musicians will have gathered to jam at the Spotted Cat. Across town National Guard trucks will patrol deserted streets, eyes out for copper thieves, as feral cats slink under raised houses, spooked by their headlights.]

Somehow, despite the clashing scenes, memory and moment, I go back to bed, fall easily to sleep. Just before dawn, a single coyote cries behind my house: three yips and a howl, then a volley of yips, followed by an almost laughing, loon-like howl. Then silence. I roll over to sleep again, my last thought before I drift away, "What a road, what a long cold road it's been."

Leaving New Orleans

It all began with my eyes. On Thursday, August 25th, 2005, fall semester just begun, my friend Catherine drove me to Metairie for the kindest cut of all: Lasik. In seconds I would leave near blindness—20/500 in my good eye—and join, for the first time since I was nine, a fully-sighted world. Catherine drove me home, Ambien tablets in my hand, hard plastic eye cups over my face. She didn't come in since I was going straight to bed. I thanked her as I shut the door; I don't remember if I waved. I would not see my friend again for four long months.

***

Four a.m., Friday, August 26th. I leap up, ripping the eye shields from my face, and greet a world of edges and sharp delineated lines. I can see my toenails and the nubble of the carpet underneath my feet. Walking through my kitchen, I can see the time glowing from my microwave, the grout between my kitchen tiles, the calendar numbers on my wall. Outside my door, in the street light's glow, I can see the veins on the leaves of the tree across my street, the grooves in the bricks of the house facing mine, the curve of hubcaps, the sidewalk's cracks. I sit until the streetlights fade and the new day breaks, in my green plastic porch chair, just looking and looking some more. Had I known that I would never sit on my porch again, I'm not sure that knowledge would have killed this joy.

***

On Saturday, I hardly leave my couch, phone in hand. The gulf is teeming with a swirling mass—the K storm—cochlear, straining toward land like batting toward a seam. We're in the cone—dead center—as the storm gains force, 3 today, by late tonight 4, and finally, on Sunday 5. There is no Category 6. The newspaper schools us in contra-flow: all lanes heading out, but there's a catch. Choose the wrong lane and there's no going back, right lanes forcing cars north to Hammond, left lanes to Baton Rouge or on to Houston and beyond. I'm memorizing flow lanes, watching the weatherman, and calling Davy all at once, while on the hour dosing my eyes.

"Hey, Davy, when are you guys leaving?"

"Not till Angela finishes up. She's working in the French Quarter. They're making her pack up all the merchandise before she can leave."

"Oh, great. I'll get back to you."

Then I call Catherine.

"Hey, Catherine, I'm getting ready to leave. I'm going to Baton Rouge. Don has an extra room. Wanna come with me?"

"No, I'm staying."

"But, Catherine, we're in the middle of the cone."

"It'll turn at the last minute; it always does. I'm staying. I'm up high; I'll be fine."

"But you've got gas and a good car."

"I've got four cats and only two carriers. I'll be fine."

"Throw the cats in the car. It's only to Baton Rouge."

"Really, I'll be fine."

"I'll call you back. Really, you need to leave."

"I'm staying. I'll be fine."

I notice a message on my phone. It's Janet, a tutor in our Learning Lab. "What are you doing? I don't know what to do. I don't know about my truck. Or that damn dog. Let me know what you're doing." I try to call her back, but her line's busy. She has no voice mail. I don't know where she lives.

In limbo, I settle back on the couch, watch the red icon spin on its projected path—straight to New Orleans—the weather channel's storm team looking grim. It's my twin brothers' birthday. They're fifty-three. I call Tom. "There's a storm in the gulf," he says. "Yeah, tell me something I don't know. Happy Birthday. Look, I'm packing up. I gotta go." I don't get around to calling Steve.

Instead, I work in the kitchen, filling bowls for the feral cat I've been feeding for a year. I've named her Mewls for her plaintive cry. She comes in through my late dog's door flap, eats, then scurries out, confirmed in her wildness. I've never gotten close enough to touch her, so there's no question of her coming along. I place an open food bag high on my table top. If water comes in, I reason, her food will stay dry. Looking back, I cringe at this failure of vision, my feeble precaution—water to the table top the most I can foresee.

I'm pacing the floor instead of packing, picturing the traffic, minute by minute feeding onto Interstate 10. I pack up my laptop, irrigate my corneal flaps, throw clothes in a suitcase, stuff documents in an envelope, call Davy again.

"You ready to leave?"

"Angela's still not finished. I'm going down there to help."

"Good plan," I say. "I'll call you back."

I try Janet again. Still busy. Then Catherine.

"Changed your mind?"

"No, but Gary's changed his. Now he wants to leave, but he doesn't have any gas. I told him he could siphon mine."

"But then you'll be really stuck. Come with me."

26

"I'm staying. I have food, water, cat food, litter. Roz and Ed are staying too. I'll be fine." I'm very close to giving up. "I'll call you back," I say instead.

The day seems endless, the TV monotonous, the phone calls increasingly moot. Another hour passes. I call Davy.

"How are you doing?"

"We got it all packed up; then Angela couldn't find her purse. She thinks she must have packed it too so we're opening boxes."

"My God. Let me know when you leave so I can leave too."

I'm getting desperate, but then so is Angela, her stress manifested in that last daft move. I pack the car, traveling light. Call Janet. It's busy still. Call Catherine. "Sure you don't want to come?" "No, I'm staying. Don't worry about me. The phones will go out and you won't be able to talk to me, but don't worry, I'll be fine." "Good luck," I say, and let her go.

The phone rings; it's Davy. "We found the purse; we're leaving." "Don't forget your cell phone," I say. "Are you coming to Baton Rouge?" "We're not sure," he answers. "We'll keep in touch." I'm out the door before the phone settles in its cradle.

As I drive away, I don't look back, not a parting glance at my house or yard, the petunias in my flower beds, the shrubs I tended. I can hardly record what I didn't do—the pain so sharp—what I didn't take, in my distraction left behind: the books, almost a thousand in all, children's books I'd saved for my grandkids, annotated college texts, a full set of Dickens—belonging to Chris—four copies of the book my mother wrote, now hard to find: *Women Pilots of World War II.* Or worse, the pictures—albums up high in kitchen cabinets, framed faces on bureau tops, but not high enough. One sweep into a pillowcase was all it would have taken. Even worse than the pictures, my mother's yearbook from World War II, *We Were Wasps*, leather-bound, women in jumpsuits smiling next to vintage planes. And hands down worst of all, what never even crossed my mind, Kate's journals, page after page in her childish, then gradually maturing hand, from second grade to now, her second year at Oberlin, a whole life in print stacked under her bed. I drove off, leaving it all, my mind on the contra flow, the cars heading outbound, chased by the storm.

***

Almost everyone who has lived through a summer and a fall in New Orleans has locked up her house, inched onto the interstate, and done that same faltering dance—stop and go, idle and surge—the wind at her back. This time is no exception. Through Metairie, the cars barely move. They crawl through Kenner. I maneuver into the outermost lane, waiting for the point where I will make my move, cross over onto I-10 East, now converted to an outbound route. Finally, past the airport, I see police cars, flashing lights, and barricades as right lanes feed to the north, left ones to the west on that emptied swath. Here, for the first time all day, I almost relax. Amazingly, I'm doing thirty; I unscrew my eye drops and throw back my head, dosing and driving, watching the world come back into focus as the moisture seeps in, evens out.

My joy returns. From the highway, I command an exotic view: cypress knees rising from stagnant pools, Spanish moss dripping from trees, flocks of egrets—white against the grays and greens—rising overhead, legs trailing behind. I can't stop looking—at the landscape, the cloud banks, the haze in the sky—or reading: highway signs, exit numbers, anything in print.

I get out my cell phone to check on Davy; they're on the road too, but headed northeast—Davy, Angela, Linda, (their dog) and a whole jazz band, The Hot Club of New Orleans, swinging toward the farthest corner of Mississippi where their violinist's wife has a home. "You sure you'll be safe in Baton Rouge?" Davy asks. "Is it far enough away?" "I'll be fine," I say, aware that I sound just like Catherine.

Two eye dosings later, I'm exiting at College Drive, toward what will become my home for a week. I've made it in evacuation record time: three hours for a one-hour drive. For tomorrow and the rest of today, my friend Don and I will stare at the rotating whirl on the TV screen—Hurricane Katrina—hell-bent for shore. As the weatherman announces each minute wobble, Don places a pin on his storm-tracker's map. Red nubs now form a gentle curve from the Bahamas, across Florida, and into the Gulf, then gradually northward toward landfall, somewhere near, just hours away. If I look beyond the red pins' course, I can see the pricks of earlier storms, freckling the map from longitude 75 east of Nassau to latitude 35 just south of Cape Hatteras, from the Yucatan north towards Brownsville and beyond. The pin holes cluster south of three Gulf states —Louisiana, Mississippi, and Alabama— rays targeting Florida from Pensacola to the Keys. Months from now Don will give me this map, expertly framed, the storm's course completed, from Atlantic to landfall (tomorrow morning) in Buras, southeast of New Orleans. Her wrath still acute, Katrina will collide with that city as a Category Three.

But Sunday night we're still in the dark. We head out for dinner, restaurants bulging with storm evacuees. I'm still riding my corneal high, drinking wine, confident that Davy and Angela are safe. After dinner, in the car, my cell phone rings. It's Chris on the line. He's frantic, panicked at Katrina's path. "Relax, Chris," I say. "Davy's way up north; I'm in Baton Rouge. We're safe." "But it's going to be awful," he replies. "People are going to die." I still can't envision the havoc he foresees. "Chris," I say, and I shudder as I write this, exact words scored in my mind: "I don't have a care in the world." As I hang up the phone, Don and I shake our heads. "That Chris," we smile.

Georges

My calm, my carefree high, with the storm poised to strike, owes much to my eagle eyes, the wine I've drunk, but even more to the ease of my escape, that pre-flight dread left unfulfilled. It was not always so. In 1998, Hurricane Georges blustering in the Gulf, I stewed on my couch for way too long, my bags all packed, unable to leave, too frightened to stay. Kate was twelve, my dog, Eightball, was alive, Catherine had just been hired, the junior Shakespearian at UNO. All over town, the native-born swaggered, full of disdain for those who had left: alarmists, fools. But as evening fell, one by one they changed their tune. Car doors began to slam, engines to start as they slunk out of town without a word. Only John, my twenty-something neighbor, thought of me. He knocked on my door, looking nothing like he often did: in full make up, heading to a gig with his 80s cover band "Bag O' Donuts." "We're leaving," he said. "You need to go too. Take Airline. The interstate's a parking lot." I thanked him, and picked up the phone.

"Catherine, we're going to Dallas. Wendy [my sister] has four bedrooms. There's lots of room for you."

"I'm staying," she answered.

"Ok," I said, too anxious to argue.

(In only a day the storm would turn to strike Biloxi—September 28th—Catherine's fortieth birthday. Alone in her apartment house on City Park Avenue, she would taste the terror and then the relief.)

But Kate and I, dog on my lap, set out in the darkness, with one goal in mind: if we can't make Dallas to at least put some miles between ourselves and the Gulf. Airline's not bad, and after some time, assuming all's clear, I make

31

what will be a near-fatal mistake: take an entrance to the interstate. What greets me there is a Bosch-like hellscape: all lanes a bumper-to-bumper creep, both shoulders lined with the cars that couldn't: overheated, hoods thrown open, passengers spilled out to wait along the highway side. My 87 Camry inches along, needle steady between hot and cold. But I'm driving a standard. After hours of this stop-and-start my left leg is shaking, my thigh in knots. I have to pee. But if I take an exit I'll lose an hour trying to get back on. I hand Eightball to Kate, and hover over a paper cup, peeing and shifting down the road.

It's well past midnight, and I'm nodding off. I turn up the radio, switch the air-conditioning to high, let it blow on my face, as I slap myself to the music's beat. So many hours, and we're still nowhere. We stop at a rest area right on the highway, walk the dog, for twenty minutes doze. Then we carry-on. Not until 1-49 will the traffic break up, my left leg be granted a reprieve. We cruise through Shreveport, through Longview, through Tyler to Dallas. It's afternoon. But Wendy has made us beds in darkened rooms where we sleep, and sleep, and sleep.

Ivan

Who would name a hurricane Ivan? To name is to create, and Ivan fulfilled its prophesy: a Terrible storm, filling up the Gulf, striking fear with its power and size, its tight rotation, the definition of its eye. Before Ivan's course was even clear, the NOAA cone yet to debut, Catherine and I decried this name, its tempting of fate, its power to invoke some Gulf god's wrath. But in September, 2004, Ivan it was, a Category Five, all Gulf states at risk.

Wendy had moved from Dallas to Park City with her daughter, Lacey, selling my refuge, so I called some motels in Baton Rouge. All full. Lafayette. All full. Alexandria, Natchitoches. Full and full. I tried Jackson. Still no luck. Then Shreveport, five hours north up the I-49. Not a bed to be had. Near desperation, I called up Del, newly retired from my college and recently married to a Shreveport prof.

"Del, I'm getting desperate here. I can't find a motel. Do you have any room?"

"Sure," she answers. "Of course Joanie's coming, and her husband, and her kids, and I think they're bringing some neighbors, and of course their pets, and maybe Janet." Wonderful Del.

"Oh, no," I reply. "You're full. I'll keep on trying."

"It'll be fun," she says. "We'll have a pajama party."

I can almost see her husband grimace in the background.

A little while later Del's back on the line with vacancies she's found just minutes from her house. I thank her profusely and call up Davy. We go through the drill.

"When are you leaving?"

"Any minute."

"Well I'm out the door."

I give him directions to one of the motels, then call up Catherine, though I know what she'll say.

"Catherine, I'm going up by Del. You sure you're staying?"

"I'm sure. I'll be fine."

"Ok, I'll keep in touch."

And I set off alone. Eightie has died. Kate's away at college. It's 1 p. m., so I'm hoping it won't be too bad. Best of all, my 99 Mazda has an automatic shift—no seized-up thighs. But despite the early hour, the interstate is worse than it was during Georges, cars backed up from my entrance at Canal to the hazy horizon hours away. It's stop and go—more stop than go—and I start to worry about Davy's car: a '92 Dodge, as yet untried. Remembering the horrorscape of Hurricane Georges, I wonder why I left first, didn't insist that they ride with me. We don't own cell phones, and I picture them stranded, Ivan churning closer and closer, picking up steam off our warm delta shores. My heart is pumping like some clutch to the floorboard. If the storm touches down while we're jammed up here, we'll scatter like Pick-Up Sticks over the marsh.

It's two a. m. before I break free past Lafayette, leave that traffic jam and sail up I-49, but I'm drifting off, so tired that even my stress can't keep me awake. I crank up the air conditioning, blare the radio in my ears, and slap myself all the way into Shreveport, then find my motel as the sun's coming up.

But something's wrong; something's very wrong. The clerk eyes me from a locked-in cage; my room is dingy, there's no hot water, and worst of all the bed is ringed by mirrors—big mirrors—one on either side, one at the foot and, to top it off, a huge framed mirror looking down from above. I'm putting some woman out of work today. I'd kill for sleep, but that bed, those mirrors. The whole room's vibe keeps me wide awake as I lie there—rigid on that

34

sleazy bed—clothes from my suitcase draped over the pillow, a towel from the bathroom draped over me. The image returns: Davy standing by the interstate, Angela asleep in the car, winds growing stronger, no help in sight. I can still see tail lights when I close my eyes, flickering as the drivers brake, then surge; brake, then surge. At last, caught in four reflecting panes, I drift off to sleep.

I'm awake two hours later, exiting that creepy bed—since I can't take a shower, watching TV. Ivan has weakened to a Category 4, looming just off Louisiana's boot. We're still in the woods. I call up Chris, but he's heard nothing from Davy. He didn't check into that nearby motel. I pace and worry and watch the TV.

Around noon, Del appears, then Janet in a beat up truck with three cages of birds and Ikey, a dog as ugly as my drive was long: a big pitbull/black lab mix. Janet didn't purchase this dog or get it from the pound; it came with her apartment. (The dog stays).

There are no more vacancies at this motel, every room filled with evacuees. Through their open doors, I can see their rooms, all beds mirror-bound, with one key difference. Only my bed has a mirror overhead. I've scored the Alpha hooker's room. I try not to contemplate why this is so.

Del invites us to a barbeque, Janet and me, plus all her house guests—animals in the backyard, free-range and caged. I feel safe and cared for. There are only three problems: Del doesn't drink, and I really need a beer; Davy's still AWOL; and that bed awaits me—its tamest tenant—for one more night. (Ivan will meet land at 2 a. m. in Orange Beach, Alabama, sparing New Orleans on its dry western side. A strong Category Three, it will wipe out my favorite hotel on the waters of Pensacola Beach, leave huge gaps in the span connecting that beach to Interstate 10).

When we wake to this news, we all head home. Davy will beat me there, having been with a drummer friend in

Baton Rouge. The weather in New Orleans is sunny and warm, those who stayed feeling justified, the rest of us once again alarmists and fools. Chris calls me to celebrate New Orleans' dodge and learn that his brother was safe all along. I'm in no mood for glee: tired, dirty, scarred by my ordeal. "That's it," I tell him. "I'm never doing this again. Next time they'll just have to bring in the body bags. I'm *never* leaving again." I will eat those words a year from now, in part because of Cindy.

Cindy

No one ran from Cindy. She was billed as a tropical storm, so we brought in our garbage cans and went to bed. It was early July, 2005, just seven weeks before Katrina would strike. But no one in New Orleans slept that night, with the screeching winds, the rain like bullets on the window panes. At first light we ventured out—the entire neighborhood in the street, sizing up the damage. The power was out, the crepe myrtles in Lakeview's sunken gardens were all destroyed, City Park had lost fifty trees, but amazingly our roofs were on, our windows intact. It was just a matter of cleaning up the limbs, the leaf-strewn street, and tending to our frazzled nerves. Over and over we said to each other: "If that was a tropical storm, I'm never staying for a hurricane!" (Months later NOAA will upgrade Cindy to just that—a Category 1 hurricane, barreling through New Orleans after striking Grand Isle, a hundred miles due south.)

Only seven weeks later—in deference to this night of wind—many from New Orleans will move their feasts to Baton Rouge, the Hot Club of New Orleans will take its gig to a neighboring state, and I will feast my eyes off College Drive, seventy-six miles from Memphis Street, one hundred and forty from where, at daybreak, Katrina will blow into Buras, LA, with one hundred twenty-five mile-per-hour winds, then turn its wrath toward North Gayoso Street, where Catherine and her four cats wait.

Black Monday

Davy was right. One hundred forty miles is only a stone's throw when a Category Three storm comes ashore. The trees in Baton Rouge toppled that night, one barely missing my car. The power went out, and we sweltered in the heat. But I got through to Catherine early that morning, her phone still working, to pass on the happy news: Katrina had missed, had swerved east to Buras, was now deflated to a Category Three. I knew before she did about the levees, the people on rooftops, trapped in attics, feeding into the Superdome. But I couldn't tell her. The phones were out by then. (Cell phones would fail us for almost a week, the 504 exchange hopelessly jammed.)

With no TV, the house a steaming box, Don and I walk through the neighborhood, climbing over fallen trees, skirting power lines, and picking up rumors about my town. A neighbor still has cable and feeds us scraps—a breached canal, a soup bowl, a sand-bag plan. But nothing is clear. Is it "overtopped" or "toppled"? Just how much water? When I ask about Lakeview, her face goes dark.

I cope through motion: breaking up tree limbs, sweeping up leaves, stuffing it all in garbage bags, and hauling them to the curb. I work for hours, purged by sweat, soothed by the rhythms of this mindless task. (For months I will move thus, wander compulsively through city streets, navigate interstates, run for miles in a limbo-state.) Days go by. The power returns, and with it TV, whose images scar. I'm worried about Catherine as pictures of looting and lawlessness loom. I go on line to list her missing, but another friend has been there first: Cynthia has logged on from upstate New York with Catherine's data—

address, occupation, cat count, health concerns. There's nothing more to do.

Chris keeps calling. "Come to DC." "We need to be together." "Davy and Angela have already left." My impulse is to follow, but I'd be giving up on Catherine, leaving her behind. Finally—torn—I succumb to his pressure, gas up my car, withdraw some cash, say goodbye, and set off again—a seasoned evacuee—leg two of my journey just begun.

Leaving Baton Rouge

This time it's not the traffic; it's the gas, more specifically, the absence of gas as I drive north, then turn east into Mississippi, whose devastation matches ours. At first I think it's an accident—the long line of motionless cars, stretching as far as the eye can see. Then it hits me: a gas line. My gauge is at a quarter tank; I probably should queue up too . But that line is barely moving. After hours of waiting, I could pull up to an empty pump. I drive past, fixated on my gas gauge, which creeps, as I drive on, to one-eighth, one-sixteenth, then I'm driving on fumes. This is worse than Georges, more horrendous than Ivan; if I run out of gas, who will rescue me now? I'll be stranded like Catherine, water to her porch top, or maybe higher, her friend headed north-east, leaving her behind. I've just concluded I deserve this fate, when a station appears with a manageable line, maybe twenty cars. Better still, an attendant—certainly one not Southern bred—is moving traffic in a seamless flow, crisp and efficient in her every move; when a pump frees up, she collects hard cash, then signals to the next car till I'm pumping too, so happy I stopped at that ATM.

There is no comfort like a just-filled tank. I can breathe again, for almost an hour, forget my cares. The world comes into focus: bills of ibises curving overhead, pine trees sharp against hazy skies, that Gulf-state shimmer making everything move. Words fill my head, a soundtrack to the pulsing scene: "And I was yet aware that this was only a moment, that the world waited outside, hungry as a tiger, and that trouble stretched above us, longer than the sky." "Sonny's Blues." In my other life, I'd be teaching this now, grading papers on my porch under leaves whose veins I could look up and see, my back to the house whose rooms I now envision—walk through in my mind—one by one, from west to east, and straight on into my back yard, conjuring up what no longer is, the words in my head not Baldwin's but mine. All the way to Chattanooga I chant and drive, aware at some level that I'm saying goodbye. Inside my hotel room I jot down those words before they can fade, then read them back. They have the rhythm of a Christopher Robin poem I read to my children when they were young. The nursery-rhyme singsong now comforts me.

Ode to a House
(A Road Poem)

I had a house, low as the sea,
Waters breached the levees and roared down my street.
I had a house.

Inside my house, low as the sea,
My living room glowed like a memory
With its Mexican blankets and desert hues,
Inside my house.

I had a kitchen, bright as a dream,
Its red walls flanked white cabinetry,
Where folk-art animals stood up high,
But still as low as the sea.
My refrigerator was a patchwork of smiles,
My table a ring of so much joy,
We'd empty a bottle, and open one more.
I had a house.

I had a bedroom, wispy and white,
My ceiling fan whirred with a friendly knock,

While down the hall where my daughter slept,
The walls remember her late-night talk.
They held the poster from her Sweet Sixteen,
And muffled her guitar and melodies.
She had a house.

Outside my house, low as the sea,
Elephant ears pushed up through the leaves,
Banana trees drooped with their heavy load,
Outside my house.
I had a porch where I'd sit and read,
Where everyone who passed by spoke to me.
Outside my house.

I have my life, and eyes that can see.
I see the desert, dry as a bone.
I'm going home. I'm going home.

It will be twenty months before I pack up my car and leave New Orleans for good. But deep inside, I'm already gone.

***

It's Monday, September 6th—Labor Day— exactly one week since Katrina's strike. I have a half-full suitcase, a gassed-up car, and 600 miles of road left ahead. Chris has mobilized all his friends. Davy and Angela have already arrived. I've only to head up 81 North, then navigate the Beltway and find Calvert Place. With my motel coffee and DC map, I drive through a world of bustle and light, trees intact, gas off every interchange, the cars around me filled with people who don't know where I've been, the woman in the Mazda, traveling light.

Just south of Roanoke, I stop at a Subway to get something to eat. My phone rings as I'm ordering—the first time it's worked in a week. It's Chris on the line. "The coast guard rescued Catherine!" he tells me. "She's in North Carolina!" I burst into tears, right in the middle of "Do you want cheese?" The counter worker hands me some napkins and calls me "Hon," just like they do back home. I can hardly count out my money and pay my bill or find my way to an empty booth, the tears that I've harbored blurring my sight. For a long time I sit in my booth and cry, the woman in the Mazda weighted like a stone. Then I wash my face, get back in my car, and drive on: toward my sons and the house in Woodley Park.

On my morning walk to get my paper, I encounter Cindy, my neighbor, her two dogs in tow. "I saw a chipmunk this morning," I tell her. "I smelled a skunk," she replies. Spring has come to Baderville.

Across the meadow all is muddy, snow patches punctuating rabbit brush and mullens, the peaks, still white-capped, looming overhead. Behind my house the hills are snow bound, but earth and dead grass encircle each tree. On long stretches of my driveway, cinders and mud have suddenly appeared. Water trickles downhill under ledges of snow and ice. Long-lost objects come to light: two sleds left behind by neighbor boys, a pair of goggles, a solitary glove. In a week or two, if the sunshine holds, I'll be driving to my house again, no longer parked in my neighbor's yard and walking up over snow and ice, hauling my groceries, lighting my path with a flashlight after dark.

Just a month ago, in the middle of a snowstorm, Cindy called to tell me the dome light in my car was on. I thanked her and said I'd just head down and check the doors. "Take a flashlight," she warned me. The wind was howling, the snow having drifted till my driveway was a ribbon, barely distinguishable from the drifts on either side. The snow stung my face as I navigated downhill, my way made clear by my flashlight and the lights of my neighbors' house. Sure enough, a car door was half-closed. I slammed it and turned to head back uphill. But even with my flashlight I could barely find my way. Cindy's house—uphill and back in the trees to my left—was all dark. Through the swirling snow, mine lay hidden too, my porch light masked by the driveway's slope. Head-down, encircled by white, I could make out my footprints, dim in the flashlight's glow. But the snow was erasing them as fast as I could follow their trail. I felt fear in my gut. Could I freeze to death on my own winding road? Be discovered in the morning by a dog or some neighbor boy, heading upward to sled down my hill? I stumbled on until, at last, my porch light would reveal, had anyone been watching, a snow-encrusted female form, reaching for the doorknob, then making it inside. From this night on I would never set out without placing a lamp before my open blinds. I would carry flashlights in my purse, in my car, and one, in miniature, on my key chain, just in case.

But today that night seems decades ago, my driveway shorter, not so steep. It's sixty degrees, not a cloud in the sky. The snow seems studded with mica chips. I miss the sound of its icy crust underneath the blades of my cross-country skis, the pull of my poles as I skate across the glinting white. Like me, two neighborhood boys have left behind their winter play. They've made a raft and are floating on the pond just south of Suzette, one fourth of it still bound by ice. Across the road waters gush through culverts as the snow melts up Rudd Tank Road. Dogs run along fences in their newly dried-out yards. Horses frisk.

I'm still alive, my first winter now a memory, the joys of my first spring all ahead.

Leaving DC

After the gibbon choruses, after the long walks to Adams Morgan and the coffee house Tryst, after the protest march and the Monk competition, I carry my suitcase down the steps of the house in Woodley Park and point my car toward Baton Rouge. It's early October, 2005—Lakeview's turn to "look and leave." But I can't do this alone. Don has packed his car with hazmat suits, face masks, water, and rubber gloves and waits for my arrival. I retrace the route I drove a month ago, picking up a pair of boots at a Wal-Mart outside Jackson.

Early on the morning of October 4th, we set out for New Orleans, dreading what we know we'll see. I've steeled myself, determined not to cry. But I'm unprepared for the colors, the smell, the lifeless swath of what was once a neighborhood of green lawns, flowerbeds, magnolias and oaks. All is ashen, leafless, in some cases gone. My sweet olive tree has fallen on my neighbor's house. On the other side, my neighbor's tree has fallen in my yard, taking out my fence. My stand of elephant ears—once as tall as I—has been reduced to an inch-high mush. My banana trees are pulpy stems, grey-brown, draped across the jumble that was once a flowering bush.

In red spray paint on my green front door, the National Guard has recorded its visit. Above my porch lights, a muddy line documents the depth of water in my house, 9.9 minus the slope of my yard, the three steps to my porch, and the threshold of my door, now swollen shut. From my porch I notice a lone spot of green. It's the tree I was gazing at a month ago in that August dawn, my new eyes making out the contours of its leaves. If this were a novel, that tree would be a symbol, but here it's just a fluke, the brackish waters kinder to some species than others.

There's no way that front door will budge, but my side door was forced in the rescue attempt of the National Guard. Now Don and I brace ourselves and look inside. My first sight is my kitchen: refrigerator on its back, blocking access to the hall; cabinets collapsed, spilling dishes on my countertops; white ceramic tiles now streaked with mud beneath the layers of books that floated in when bookcases toppled in bedrooms and hall. Between the ceiling and the water line, a polka dot strip of 3-d mold wraps around the room, like some paper hanger's handiwork, perfectly level. My kitchen clock still ticks overhead. It's worse than I imagined, but I'm not completely dispossessed. On top of my cabinets, dry and untouched, stand six folk-art animals who watched it all: two Navajo sheep, a Polish ram, a Navajo eagle, a Guatemalan bird and wolf. In Lakeview, the waters must have risen gently, unlike in the Ninth Ward, where houses traveled down the block and cars flipped upside down. Here, there's not a broken dish, my animals upright, exactly as I left them.

Climbing over the refrigerator we step down onto a sodden mass—the fallout from those bookcases, their fiction now, quite literally, pulp. The mattresses on beds have resettled askew, Kate's balanced on her footboard, mine tilted too, our comforters, once white, now streaked with brown. Mud stains the faces of Kate's high school class, smiling out from the poster on her closet door. It masks the messages those same people wrote beneath her baby picture at her Sweet Sixteen. I can't bear to bend and look under her bed.

More drama awaits in the laundry room. My washer and dryer, once side-by-side, have converted to a stacked set, the dryer, on the bottom, having floated down first. Shoes spill out from my closet, where clothes hang, mud-stained, bearing a smell I could never wash out. Some fabrics—three weeks steeped in a toxic brew—now tear away in my hands. The rest of my clothes will lie casketed forever in a face-down bureau, whose contents don't merit the effort it would take to right it and hatchet open its drawers.

Every step I take falls on more sodden books. Every wall bears the same black-mold strip. Every room holds a new shock: the tarry pool of water trapped in my bathtub, the upside-down computer table, the couch, spun half circle to face the wall. Yet even here there are glimpses of beauty: the patterns of growths on slipcovers, their colors—salmon and lime green—the lacey profusion in my salad bowl.

But even for my eyes, there's too much to see. We gather up the dishes, the animals, the Mexican blankets, the pictures, and the WASP book, and load up the car—having looked, now ready to leave. Taking one glance back, I notice a message on my neighbor's house. In red spray paint, the Guard has drawn a cross and written underneath the single word: "CAT." On the ground below lies a sunken black shape. Mewls. I feel sad, but it's hard to mourn for a feral cat when holes in roofs mark my neighbors' escapes, the rest of their story still untold. I will learn in time of deaths just around my block, old women in their attics too weak to break through, thus dying there from the August heat. I leave Mewls where she lies, climbing back in the car.

The smell of my house rides with us to Baton Rouge, calling to mind trips I took as a child, we five in the back seat, my father, a limnologist, driving the car—one eye on the road, the other on the landscape. Spotting a pond, he would haul out his net and seine for fairy shrimp or copepods, then send the scent of pond scum back to us as he stowed his gear. This smell is different, though, less biotic, catching in the throat.

Back in Don's backyard I lay out the blankets, newly washed, the Clorox-soaked dishes, to dry in the sun. I air out my animals. I sort through my pictures, the centers often clear, as colors, bleeding from the edges, stopped shy of some smiling face. The WASP book is a miracle. Its leather cover must have swollen under water, then sealed shut, preserving the pages inside. I leaf through to my mother's face: a formal portrait with her wings and beret; next a candid shot: one foot on her airplane's wing, about to embark on a solo flight. In the picture I like best, my mother, hands in her pockets, grins, as beside her a young male instructor grins back.

A hard day ends. I glance back over the yard where they lie, they dry, they air in the sun—the survivors—(and I one).

***

In the morning Don and I pick up my photos from a drugstore nearby. The streets are jammed, as they will be for months to come. It seems half of New Orleans has moved to Baton Rouge, has set up housekeeping, enrolled children in schools, or transferred from Delgado to BRCC just down the road from College Drive. Those pictures document my damage—the holes in my roof, my toppled fence—for the Farmers adjuster who will, in time, nickel and dime away the money for my loss. But I don't know this now. Instead, I'm in for a surprise. At the start of the roll, I find six early-August shots. They document a festive night: Ringed round my table sit Catherine, Angela, Davy, and Wendy—in town from Utah—meeting Davy's wife for the very first time. In one, a puppy-Linda sits propped up on her mistress's lap. Everyone smiles behind plates now emptied of the salmon I served with a cold dill sauce, two wine bottles drained at the table's edge, all glasses full. The pictures capture a life now gone, a Big Easy moment, juxtaposed with the rest of the roll: my new life in grey. I will cherish these shots—this feeble record of my pre-storm home. Months from now I will add to them a picture that today I don't know still exists, high and dry on my office desk in Building One. There, Chris, Kate, and Davy flash disheveled smiles on Christmas day.

In time, Kate will tell me her own consolation tale. In late July, just weeks before that salmon feast, she and her boyfriend spent their day reading her journals aloud on her bed—laughing at her childish prose, then hearing her, as years passed, finding her voice. What is gone, what Katrina stole, for Kate thus remains, captured in a mental flash, some words, whole lines, still scored in her mind. In New Orleans, we treasure whatever we have—hand held or recalled—our slivers, our scraps.

That night Don and I add to the crush in a restaurant nearby. Half-way through our meal, my phone rings from the booth where we sit. It's Daf, an old high school friend, who sent me a check when she heard of my loss: a thousand dollars, no strings attached. Now, she wants to know my plans. I'm going to Flagstaff; I'm tired of being someone's guest; I've never seen Mt. Humphreys in the fall. She offers to help me drive. Phone propped on her shoulder, she searches for flights, while I grin across at Don and finish my wine. "There's one to George W. Bush Airport in Houston," she says. "Can you pick me up there?" "George W. Moron Bush Airport?" I answer. "Sure." Offended, she lays down the terms: no politics and no religion, safe-talk for 1200 miles, Houston to Phoenix, where she'll pick up her car and drive up to Payson, while I take the main road to Flagstaff, then beyond.

Daf. In middle school we spent our weekends running around the high school's track, two budding jocks, barefooted, years before the sneaker craze, the jogging fad,

50

the validation of Title Nine. We'd leap into the broad-jump pit, marking our landings with sticks we'd found, then sail beyond, new records set. In the summers, we'd ride our bikes to the pool and spend two hours with our life-guard coach, who taught us to tuck, to pike, to lay-out over the waters of Tempe Beach. Born too early, decades too soon. Surely we can drive in peace across Texas, through New Mexico and on into our home state: a Christian Republican, an atheist Democrat, Thelma and Louise both holding our tongues.

In the morning Don and I pack my Survivors and store them in his extra room. I scrape the Kerry sticker off my bumper and set off for Houston to pick up my friend. We stop in San Antonio, safe-talk along the Riverwalk, through dinner, and, the next day, over the pancake of Texas's plains. Daf drives with an inborn expertise. She was backing into carports before the rest of us could angle park. For hours it rains, but she maintains her speed, relaxed at the wheel, while I breathe in the greasewood scent, and feel I've come home. When I drive, Daf, a realtor, is busy on her cell; she's clinched two deals before we reach the state line. "Wow, you're doing well," I say. "Yes," she replies. "God has been really good to me this year." She's broken our pact, but I let it go. Three Christmases from now I will give back her thousand-dollar gift when she's suffering through the housing bust. But today it's she that's riding high.

We part in Phoenix, my true-blue friend, Katrina having once again lavished gifts. Daf drives through Mesa to Route 87 and her rim-country home. I head through Phoenix on I-10 West, then take the exit for 17 North. The sky is cloudless, the air smog-free, as I set out on this uphill road, my vision honed by the desert air. In three hours I will have climbed from eleven hundred to seven thousand feet, then three hundred more as I drive through Flagstaff to the house on Hawk Hill Road. Up each hill, around each rise,

51

new scenes unfold. First, giant saguaros and teddy bear cholla stud the buttes above the Valley of the Sun. Then suddenly, around one bend, they all disappear. Now prickly pears spread out across a high plateau. Then, higher still, their grey-green mingles with the darker green of juniper shrubs until all cacti vanish and shrubs become trees. I feel as if I'm watching a curtain call, the minor players bowing first, then moving corner-stage as those with bigger roles accept their applause. At last, from the wings, the leads appear and bow low, center-stage, the audience rising to its feet. I'm well outside of town when the stars appear: ponderosa pines, erect against the backdrop of the San Francisco Peaks. The air's so thin there's nothing between them and me. I can see the mottling of their trunks, cinnamon on ash, their needles pointed toward the sky.

I pick up groceries in town, then head out 180, past the Ski Lift Lodge, to the vacant house on Hawk Hill Road. A week ago, on Memphis Street, I didn't cry, but I tear up now as I drive up my road. Time has passed, but nothing has changed, from the splintered deck to the carport's sag. Inside, clothes still hang in closets. My children's drawings, circa 1988, still hang on the refrigerator door. From the depths of my secular soul, I can feel my parents' presence here, especially my mother's, she who envisioned this house, made a model out of cardboard, drove up to Flagstaff and purchased the land, then helped drive every nail, lay every tile. I am Mrs. Bast from *To The Lighthouse* (another book I'd be teaching now), reentering the house left vacant ten years while a world war raged and its mistress died: "There were boots and shoes; and a brush and comb left on the dressing table, for all the world as if she expected to come back tomorrow." I am Lily Brisco, gripped by that loss: "To want and not to have—to want and want—how that wrung the heart, and wrung it again and again." I could use my mother's comfort now. But she's sheltering me still, this house she designed and built, one-fifth mine.

It's cold inside. Cob webs dangle from the loft, to the pine-tree beams, and down to the very sofa and chair that furnished the house where we all grew up: 2015 Sierra Vista, outside Phoenix in the suburb Tempe. Upstairs, the bedroom set is older still—bought in the fifties back in Louisville, where we lived before my father got the job at ASU. My mother's dishes fill the cupboards, her linens a tiny closet upstairs; my father's service cap from World War Two hangs from a pine-pillar next to the stove. It's all too much. But I settle in, establish a routine.

In the mornings I build a fire. I find an old radio and pick up NPR. I buy the paper at the Ski Lift Lodge. One morning I look out to see a woman pushing a wheel barrow up my road. It's Cindy, bringing me wood. She buys me fire-starters—paraffin squares that instantly ignite, then burn for ten minutes under my logs. She invites me over to her house in the trees where I meet the neighbors, a self-reliant lot who built their own homes, who plow their own driveways, tend their horses, split their wood. When I show them pictures of my flooded home, they take me in: a human version of Edna, the Res dog, rescued by Cindy up on Navajo land.

Still craving motion, I spend my days exploring the state, driving down to Sedona just to look at the rocks, then north to Wupatki, an Indian dwelling quite literally ruined. In 1924 President Coolidge established this place as a monument, in the process driving its residents out: "...their livelihood was in competition with ranchers, and later inconsistent with the mission of the National Park Service," the Visitor Center explains. One of these residents, Elsie Tohonnie, records her displeasure at having to leave: "I still want to live where we once lived. I also want to be compensated for my loss, being made to move out. I never consented to the establishment of the park." Still another former resident describes that same pain: "I try not to think about those days. My grandson tells me, 'It is gone. Now try to think of what you can do every day.'" I connect with these people, these evacuees, banished from their desert home, so people like me can stand back and look. I think of New Orleans, its projects padlocked for the greater good, while residents languish in Houston and beyond. How little it takes to signify "home." I can picture myself happy here, living in one tiny room whose vista expands its walls to take in miles of scrub and sky. I could throw down a sleeping bag under some ledge if it meant waking up to skies like these. As I leave, I sign the visitor's book, pausing for a moment to remember who I am. In the end I write, instead of my name: "Katrina evacuee in search of beauty. Thank-you."

On the way back I stop at Sunset Crater, whose black cone rises over lava fields where salmon-colored pentstemmon thrive on ash. (How little it takes to put down roots.) In the sixties we climbed this cone, then ran back down with cinder-filled shoes. Now, the path is closed, the crater preserved. To compensate, there's Lennox Crater nearby, with a wide-carved path, across from a lot where I park my car. At 7,000 feet, the climb is a challenge; I pause three times before I reach the top. There, I gaze down into the cone, rimmed round with trees under that same sky. Feeling its draw, I walk into the hole. But when I climb out, I can't find the trail back down. I've come up wide to the left or right, which way I can't tell. I search for awhile, and then give up—opting for the certainty of "down." I'm tearing up the soil as I half-walk, half-slide in a desperate trail-braid to find my car. But when I'm finally down, there's nothing but lava as far as I can see—a charred-black sea—straight ahead, to the left, and to the right, behind me the crater, above me the sky. I'm very near panic; I could wander forever over those fields, until buzzards dropped down to pick my bones clean. Again I look to the right, to the left—where I pick up a glint, as if some hiker were signaling the rescue crew. But it's I who am saved: the sun's reflecting off my car in the lot some two hundred yards from where I stand. I stop at the Visitor Center on the way out, and tell them they need to mark their trail. They give me a look I will see again as I try to doff my urban ways. Their eyes say, "No one could miss that path," but I did, so others could. Or could they? I slink out, feeling ashamed.

Inside, I'm out of my element too. My fires are smoky; at night I'm outwitted by mice. I hear the trap spring but wake to find neither bait nor mouse. I'd leave them alone, but at night they scuttle in the wall behind my bed, a washboard percussion that troubles my dreams. I'm afraid of hanta virus; if infected through their droppings, I could die in days. At the Ski Lift Lodge I seek out solutions from seasoned pros. "Peanut butter," they all agree, slathered on so that in prying it loose the mouse will linger, positioned to die. A white-haired man hunched over his beer then segues into a tragic tale. One day, while in town, his house on Hart Prairie burned to the ground when pack rats gnawed wires, igniting the blaze. This man and I thus share a bond. We leave mice behind and start in on insurance woes. When we introduce ourselves, he shakes my hand: "I knew your parents," he tells me. "I met them in the 80's at a dinner party at Carothers' house, up behind you in the woods." Imagine, I think, if my parents could have seen ahead—almost thirty years—to this strange night: their daughter and their friend, Bob, both bereft, meeting at the very Lodge they stayed at while they built their house. After long days framing in the mountain sun, they must have sat thus—maybe in these very seats—like us now, telling stories, drinking beer. Two years from now, from these self-same stools, I will introduce Bob to my daughter,

55

Kate. "You have your grandmother's eyes," he'll say. "No one's ever told me that," she'll answer, surprised. Only Bob, who knew my mother but not Kate's father, could see in that blue a binding thread, a recessive gene passed down through me. When we pull up roots, we lose these links, these witnesses: our school-yard friends who've known our parents as long as we, our parents' friends who knew us before we knew ourselves, who watched us grow. By design we move away, or by circumstance scatter—Davy and Angela now in Brooklyn, Catherine back home in upstate New York, Ninth Warders holed up in Houston or beyond, one Lakeview lady at the Ski Lift Lodge, perched on a barstool, imagining her parents perched there too.

It's late October, the days growing short. Snow and aspen leaves litter the trails, especially my favorite up on Agassiz, its name but two letters from our Gulf-state bane: "Katrina to Kachina," I think, as I hike, until an urban-bred panic grips my heart and I book it back out. I drive down to Payson and hike with Daf, one grandchild attached to my hand, the other in a pack on her grandmother's back. I wander through the town, discovering galleries and coffee bars.

One night I stop in at Cindy's for pizza. It's dark when I leave. "I'll walk you, home," she offers, flashlight in hand. We pick our way over cinders and rocks, down the slope toward the road leading up to my house. As we leave the trees, I look up, gasp, then fall—over grass tufts, onto cinder dust, a large rock bashing my shin through my jeans. The sky has thrown me: so dark, its stars so bright, the Milky Way barreling through it all. For the first time I understand "Starry Night." There is drama, motion, almost music in that sky, a synesthesia that has toppled me. For weeks my leg will ache, every throb recalling that night. Two months later, back in New Orleans, I will tell my colleagues of that sky, that fall. "Oh, yes," Nancy will answer. "I fell too. And Cathy fell on the Westbank, walking to the parking lot. She has a hair-line fracture of the jaw. And Tim—have you seen his cast? A broken wrist. It's Katrina Falling Syndrome. Survivor's guilt. We hurt ourselves because the storm didn't hurt us enough." Intrigued, I call up Kate. "Are you crazy?" she says. "How could you have survivor's guilt? You lost everything you had." I did, but it's not enough to cancel out my odyssey: my days on the road with brand-new eyes, my walks through the Capital, my mountain hikes, my desert drive, Wupatki, Sedona, that crater climb, my one-fifth mountain home, the lodge (its ghosts), the girlhood friend, the survivors (and I one), a catalogue of excess juxtaposed with dearth—the rooftops, the Superdome, the bodies in the flood.

It's mid-November, cool becoming cold. One morning at Macy's, my favorite coffee house, I gaze out the window to see snow start to fall—big wet flakes that stick to the sweatshirts of college students walking by, to the bright yellow leaves of the tree across the street. For a long time I watch the snow, melting as it hits the ground, but magical in its journey there. When I drive back to Baderville, three hundred feet assert themselves: There's snow everywhere, a pristine coat on the road to my house, a dusting on my roof, a thin veneer on my railings and deck. It's time to leave. A few nights later, I pack my car (still traveling light), in the morning turn off the hot water and pump, set the propane to fifty degrees, close all the blinds and lock the doors. My neighbor, Karen, has left me a note and a bag of road snacks for my trip. I drive off early, while everyone sleeps. But I've told them all that I'll be back. And I will: eighteen months from now, in early June, 2007, after locking up my FEMA trailer and packing my Mazda with all that I own. I'll retrace the route that Daf and I drove, this time with my daughter, Kate, across Texas, through New Mexico, and on up to Flagstaff, then seven miles beyond: to my new old home, the house on Hawk Hill Road.

On April seventh, I climb on a ladder and knock the last bit of snow from my roof, an icy soul patch, three feet square, that has out-clung every other crust. I am now, officially, the last house in Baderville to stand snow-free (not counting a stubborn spot on my deck or the glacier in my driveway that might not melt till June). From my window, the meadow stretches, yellow and brown, to the mountain's skirt, a deep pine green that climbs up to meet rock, then snow-tipped peaks.

The bluebirds are back, posing high on mullens, my feeder a crush of nuthatches, juncos, grosbeaks, and jays. Along the road I see swallows and sparrow hawks, in the woods the white rumps of red-shafted flickers, on the rooftops ravens, hawks overhead. Any day now the elk will return to move behind me, ghost-like, in the forest after dark. My mother, who named our street, could just as well have chosen Elk Hill Road. Now and then they jump the fence and graze in the field just west of the house. They wander across highways from dusk to dawn. I both miss them and wish they'd never return.

In late September I was driving at dusk to a film-series screening at NAU. Just past the lodge, I dimmed my high beams for another car that was coming my way. In an instant I felt surrounded by dusk, as if a screen had been thrown up, blocking my view. Then the circuits sparked in my slow-cranking brain: elk! Just a few feet before me, the huge beast was crossing the road, its grey-brown flank like a piece of the night. I slammed on my brakes and blew my horn to warn the driver in the other lane. We both thus avoided a fatal wreck: an elk through the windshield, antlers in our laps.

Just a few days later, the propane man was checking my tank. Looking back in my woods, he said, "The elk will be bugling soon. You'll hear them back here." I was grateful for his warning. That new word, "bugling," would explain the sound I'd awaken to a few weeks hence, a banshee cry that would jolt me from my sleep and freeze my limbs, till I'd remember elk could trumpet like that. One night, the bugle boys jammed till dawn, a dominant male protecting his girls. At the lodge the next day, a neighbor, Tammy, asked me, laughingly, how I'd slept. "Not great," I replied. "I figured," she said. "I felt like I was hitting the snooze button all night long!" This bugling would continue through October and beyond, a little night music piped through the trees.

After the elk mating season ends, I take my car to the DMV and change my plates, cementing my commitment to my mountain home. I mail in Louisiana IHB-188 and screw on Arizona 327-ZEH. In New Orleans, Catherine and I would read these plates like metallic tea leaves, uncovering a self-revealing phrase. It was she, a wizard at cracking the code, who saw in my old one, "I Hate Bush." Now I send her an email enlisting her help. "Catherine," I write. "I can't figure out my new license plate. I'm coming up empty with that 'Z'". In a nanosecond she emails back: "It's either Zen Enlightenment Hiking or Zillions of Elk Howling." Elk howling it is. Or maybe, I think with a shudder, "Zillions of Elk to Hit."

This same week of April the mountain closes, the lifts shut down, as the city reacquaints itself with spring-time sports: mountain biking, climbing, hiking on the snow-free trails. To mark the moment, a group of skiers takes a last run down Agassiz—naked in the frigid air. Elk droppings show up on forest roads. Tiny flowers poke through ash. Winter's past. In the meadow first, then up the hills, it all starts over again.

Kate's Bedroom

The Kitchen with the Wall Clock Still Ticking

Blue Tiles

In My Livingroom

My House Being Bulldozed

My New Neighborhood

Abandoned Car

Ninth Ward Church

Enter and Be Shot.

House on Hawk Hill Road

The Peaks from My Deck

My Fire

After Skiing

Leaving Baderville, 2005

This time I choose the northern route, through Albuquerque and Dallas, then down to New Orleans on I-49. I can stay the second night in Shreveport with Del. Even better, I'll pass through that stretch of I-40 where the arrow-straight road will throw up mirages, the red rocks glow, in a pure distillation of the desert West. In my mind I'll hear a soundtrack custom made for a scene like this, a song by Myshkin, who moved to New Orleans after living north of Santa Fe, in a little town called Chimayo: "Oh the West is where you go when you're running away/It's the last long road, it's the great escape/It's a big, blazing icon of the last free space/Sometimes it lives up to its myth that way." When the song fades, in my rear-view mirror the landscape shrinks, I'll resign myself to Texas and its colorless plains, then New Orleans, where even the oaks will have lost their charm.

I'm getting gloomy, a residual of 9.9. But I perk up after my night with Del. She tells me her grandson lost his house too, but has bought a gutted one just blocks from mine, that people are returning, life limping along. We walk through her neighborhood, rehash old times, then say good-bye as I point my Mazda toward the Gulf and home.

It's just as always, this low-slung land—egrets by the roadside, pendant clouds, oppressive air—until west of New Orleans, the damage appears. Along the interstate, in Metairie, whole sides of buildings gape, innards exposed. Blue tarps cover roofs. Businesses stand empty, employees gone. But over the 17th Street Canal, true horror waits. This can't be my town. Who are these people, camped out on the bayou? In tent encampments under overpasses? Sleeping in their own front yards? Across from Delgado, National

Guard trucks line the neutral ground where litter piles soar
—more than litter—whole living rooms, (a sodden mass),
bedroom sets, mattresses, (that smell that rode along to
Baton Rouge), kitchen ware, clothes, appliances, toys. The
houses wear their trauma on their siding and doors, the
spray-paint code of the National Guard, then sometimes a
reply, in a new form of storm-chat evolved through need:
"We're coming home," "Cats Being Fed," "One Dead Dog,
Owner Will Bury," or darker still, the epitaph in red paint
for all to see, "One Dead in Attic," the title now of a book
by Chris Rose. Just as bad are the abandoned cars, four or
five per block, like coffins themselves. I turn left on
Toulouse, and into the driveway of Davy's house.

In a way things have worked out for Davy and me. I
still have a job, but have lost my house. He still has a house
but has lost his job—or jobs: the Sunday brunch gig at
Windsor Court, the Friday night gig at d.b.a., then across
town that same night the later gig at Windsor Court, the
teaching at NOCCA , the private lessons, all gone in a puff
the morning Katrina blew into town. He was booked for
two sets at Snug Harbor that Sunday, just nine hours before
the storm would arrive. By then, he was throwing down
drinks with the Hot Club some three hundred fifty miles
away. I'm grateful for my job, the spring semester just two
months hence, and for these walls that will house me in this
interlude while FEMA sets up our trailer park and three
men of better means will move in here.

The door opens easily; the carpet is dry—not a leak, not
a seep under windows or doors. The refrigerator has been
cleaned and disassembled by Davy and Angela just weeks
ago when they traveled back here to pick up their gear
before returning to settle in Brooklyn's Crown Heights. I
locate the lights, make up a bed, pick up a chew toy Linda
has left. I try not to cry, but that chew toy encapsulates a
life now gone: Davy and Angela just six-months married

with their new rescue-puppy when it all came apart. I'm anxious too. The street is dark; I don't know the neighbors — those few who've returned—I'm leery of the strangers who've moved into town; there's no police presence; my mind still harbors TV footage of desperate looters after the storm. I check the windows, check, then recheck, all the doors. I sleep, wake, sleep, wake until morning arrives.

In the daylight I can see what the storm winds wrought. A strip of shingles has blown off the roof, along with the vent cap. At least three trees from neighboring yards now fill the backyard, their branches and leaves obscuring the fence. In the front yard, the waters have killed all the plants except, inexplicably, one rose bush. Kate's car, an ancient Mitsubishi she adored, sits flooded out front.

In Mid-City, I notice, houses lined up side by side have suffered widely varying fates, unlike in Lakeview where none escaped. Across the street one of four houses stands, like Davy's, high and dry. The other three have taken on water, less than my house, three or four feet, but even inches can destroy a home. Up the block my colleague Cathy (Katrina Falling Syndrome fractured jaw) had to move from hers when only eight inches seeped through the door. I go back inside, collect my purse, and walk up three blocks to Carrollton for a cup of coffee at City Perk.

I'm shocked to see there boarded-up buildings, water lines, windows frosted with post-storm grime. It never occurred to me that even here Katrina would have left her mark. During rainstorms, when water would block my route, I could count on Carrollton to get me through. But this road was no match for a levee break. Now a festive corridor has lost its glow. Not just City Perk, but Venezia's, Angelo Brocato's, New York Pizza, Juan's Flying Burrito— all stand lonely in the morning sun. I walk back to Davy's and get my car. I'm desperate for community. There must be some place immune to this gloom. But it's much the same for a couple of miles—businesses boarded, water lines like bathtub rings, moldy discards heaped by the road.

Finally, almost to the river, at Oak Street I find it, a Rue de la Course with cars outside. Almost every table there is filled with people who look like me: disheveled, slightly shell-shocked, comrade-deprived. There are coffee and some pastries, but styrofoam cups and plastic spoons: too few employees for a dish-washer. I buy a paper and sit by the window, trying to regain that Big Easy ease. But something's wrong, and it's not just the styrofoam. It takes me awhile to figure it out: There's not a child to be seen, not a teenager, not a college student, nothing but adults wherever I look–time-worn adults—in their forties and fifties, reading their papers unperturbed. The twenty-somethings have transferred to colleges out of town; the younger students have done so too, moved out with their parents—the thirty-somethings absent here—leaving us: a whole town of greybeards in a deep-South Hamlin too sad for words. I can't shake this feeling as I drive back up Carrollton cushioned by quiet—no children playing, no teenagers blaring their music as they drive off to their Uptown schools, PJ's coffee perched on the dash.

Instead of going home, I turn right on Esplanade to North Gayoso and the big blue house where Catherine stayed for that lonely week, marooned with her cats. She had food and water but grew fearful of the roving gangs, their gunshots sounding so near one night that she signaled with a flashlight from behind her blinds until a Coast Guard helicopter swooped down to haul her up, leaving all four cats behind. I spot two now, Elsie on the porch by the rocking chair and Naughty Guy skulking under the house. Food and water bowls attest to the care of the next-door neighbors who stayed behind. I call up Catherine to relay the news, a witness to the health of at least these two. She sounds relieved, but is still too traumatized to come back

71

here. She's bought a truck—obsessed with height as I with motion, each of us coping in her cryptic way.

Back at Davy's house I work outside in a futile counter to all-out ruin. I pick up tree limbs, glass shards, metal strips, brackets, nails—doohickeys and thingamabobs—all manner of matter I can't even name, torn loose from roofs, stripped from gutters, blown and floated, then washed up here. I sweep, I scrape, I tidy my tiny city blot, but it's like scooping sand into a sieve. One gust of breeze, one relief truck, one resident returned and it's all resifted: a debris-diffusion of epic scope.

From across the street, a neighbor appears. He's Johnny, he says, and I need a tetanus shot if I'm going to be digging in this toxic dirt. I look down at my hands, grime-encrusted, but free of nicks. I thank him for the warning just the same, then realize that in these hours of work I've seen no birds, encountered no beetles, no roaches, not a worm, not even an ant. In this modern-day Hamlin, the very soil has given up ghosts. No rats, no children, and tomorrow, I decide on the spot, there will be no me. I need to move on. There will be time enough for sadness next term, a full-impact sadness felt in the bones.

Leaving New Orleans

On November 20th I pack my car and drive off again, now bound for Brooklyn where another old friend has reentered my life. Anthea, from my college days, has invited us all to her house for Thanksgiving. She lives in a tony section of that borough, in Park Slope, just blocks (and worlds) from Davy in Crown Heights.

After two days of driving, I stop at Oberlin to pick up Kate. Together we navigate toll roads and tunnels, entrusting Map Quest to broker our way. It leads us into Chinatown, promising Canal Street, then Brooklyn by way of the Manhattan Bridge. Instead, we end up in a maze of streets—bus-congested, every face foreign, the bustle and noise jarring loose the memory of gazing out at that charred black sea. We're hopelessly lost, and I'm coming unhinged. "Mom," Kate tells me, "you've got to calm down." She's right, but such moments tap into a deep-seated angst bred of wind and high water, then exile from my comfort zone. It's as if I've left Hamlin to encounter Oz. But here it will take more than heel-taps to save me. Alongside my Mazda, pedestrians, buses, taxis and cops all move as if tossed in a giant wok. Just as I'm despairing, my agent of deliverance arrives on the scene: that laser-bearing wizard whose handiwork, quite literally, now sees me through. Down a narrow street I make out a sign with an arrow and the welcome words, in perfect focus, "Manhattan Bridge." I follow its lead to another sign and then—Eureka!—up onto the bridge. Across the water, I feed onto Flatbush, inch through traffic, then turn down Davy's downtrodden block, where for fifteen days I'll become a New Yorker, Big Easy to Big Apple with a little stir-fry in between.

Thanksgiving brings together two old friends, Anthea's husband, two of her children and two of mine, plus Sam, reader of those under-bed journals, minus Angela, who's visiting her parents in Brazil, and Chris, who's with Elena in DC . Anthea has made here an enviable home, a three-story brownstone filled with warmth, and an enviable life, which she shares with me. We eat Dim Sum, then see "The Producers"; we navigate the subway into Manhattan, then take in a concert at Carnegie Hall. I can almost picture myself living here, till these hard-core urbanites make me see that I come from a little laid-back town. On my own, I'm flummoxed by the subway grid. As I walk the dog, I watch my back. Most of all I'm irked by that twice-a-week shuffle where at prescribed times we repark our cars—all jockeying for spaces on alternate sides—so the street-cleaning truck can sweep the block.

Somehow Davy has adapted. He drives his car right into the city and finds a parking place next to his gig. He chooses the right bridge to take him home. I ride along, carefree—into Midtown, East Village, Soho, Tribeca—where he joins two musicians far from home, like him from New Orleans, all playing the long odds of making it here. For awhile two members of The Hot Club were holed up in Brooklyn too, contemplating settling in. But eventually they went back home, the life too hard here, leaving only Davy, who's fallen in now with another musician, from the upper Ninth Ward. She's Linnzi Zaorski, a platinum version of Betty Boop who sings jazz standards in retro-attire. She could catch on here, I think as I watch them, Linnzi backed by Davy, Mark Anderson and Scott Bourgeois, a Big Easy combo, the crowd all smiling, leaving tips. But in time she too will return to New Orleans and the d.b.a. on Frenchmen Street. Only Davy will stay behind.

It's time for Kate to go back to school. I opt to drive her —across the Verrazano Bridge (as far away from

Chinatown as I can get), then from Staten Island onto Highway 180, and ten hours later into Oberlin. We unload her gear, then go out to dinner at the best place in town: a swanky little restaurant with private booths, soothing lights and tasty Asian-fusion fare. I feel the tension in my shoulders ease until I order wine and am denied. "It's Sunday," the waiter says. I'm shocked but answer, "Then I'll just have a beer." Denied again, I lose it. "This is *not* a theocracy," I say, too loud, then am instantly ashamed for behaving this way. I fret and fume my way through dinner, now feeling myself that Big Easy draw, its Latin culture, its disdain for rules. I see for the first time that, like those musicians, I've become a product of its easy vibe—and also, since Katrina, that I'm way too into alcohol. Two months from now, back at work, I'll discover my colleagues have been drinking too, some taking up smoking, while abandoning their diets and exercise routines. After working registration, I'll say to Brad, my colleague sitting next to me, "Boy, I'm exhausted!" "That's because it's the first time we've been upright in months," he'll laughingly reply. But it's true. We're falling apart in more ways than one.

In the morning I say good-bye to Kate and get back in my car. "Mom, this is crazy, you know," she says as I leave. And she's right; it is. I could have put her on a bus. But it's working for me: the movement, the hours alone, the time spent sitting in my Mazda home. Across Ohio, across Pennsylvania, and back into New York state I drive. But as I cross the bridge, I become confused. I don't know which exit will take me back to Davy's. If I wait too long, I'll be funneled out of Brooklyn and right back into New York. I choose the next exit, drop down onto city streets, where— on bicycles, on sidewalks, in every car—Chinese faces peer out at me. I've done it again. I'm stuck in some nightmare, some urban version of "Groundhog Day." I pull over, get out of my car and pick out a friendly face, a middle-aged man with a little girl. "I'm lost," I say. "I'm trying to get to Brooklyn and have ended up in Chinatown." With that very same accent I'd hear in New Orleans, he laughs and says: "You're in Brooklyn, darlin'. Brooklyn has a Chinatown too!" Then he points me toward Prospect Park, an easy shot from Davy's street. As I drive away, the little girl asks, "What was wrong with that lady?" And this is funny— objectively I can see this is funny—but I can't seem to laugh, the joke on a much-too-frazzled me.

It's early December, my journey winding down. But there's one more person I need to see: my oldest friend, Laure, who lives near the mayor on the upper East side. We met in fourth grade, our friendship assured on the day our teacher was defining "cargo," and Laure raised her hand. "Could gasoline be cargo?" she asked with a grin. "Yes, it could," replied the teacher. "I thought so," Laure answered, "because it makes a car go." That's the only time I ever saw that teacher laugh or even smile, and I was wowed. This girl was for me.

Now I study the subway map to find my way to visit her. From the A line I'll transfer to the 4/5 line, then get off at Lexington, count off the streets up to 82nd and walk due east. She's right on the river. If I get my feet wet, I'll have gone too far. It's a long haul from that subway stop, but I can do a grid, the avenues all crossing streets. As I wait for a light, a young couple approaches and asks for directions. "I'm from New Orleans," I explain, as I did three months ago outside Tryst. "Oh, we're from Venice, on the Delta," they reply. "How'd you do in the storm?" "I lost my house," I answer, to be met with, "So did we! Isn't it sad?" I agree that it is, then wish them luck as they fade back into the sidewalk's crowd. "Did that really happen?" I wonder, amazed. We're everywhere—we evacuees— disoriented, houseless, culture-shocked, yet no one can see us. Somehow we blend: from Houston to Atlanta, from

Brooklyn to Manhattan, riding subway cars down into the darkness, then climbing back up into the light. Wherever I go, I feel emblazoned, as if bearing in storm-code a scarlet "K." But in truth, I'm unmarked, though emitting some signal so that (twice now) inexplicably—at that DC party, on these crowded streets—I've drawn fellow sufferers. Like pain-seeking missiles, they find their mark.

Laure's apartment on the seventeenth floor looks down on the river where bridges splay over barges and tugboats far below. I remember the fate of Clapton's son who tumbled out a window just like these, the ones I'm gazing out of now, as the daylight fades and water glows. I wonder how Laure could dare to raise a child up here. The last time I visited, Betsy was seven; now she's cross-town in college at NYU. It's been too long, and would have been longer had the storm path veered, or the Corps built our levees up to code. Again, I'm conflicted by the double whammy that brought me here.

When it's time to leave, Laure puts me in a cab—no riding the subway alone at night. It might be years before I see her again. But tonight I'm sated. In the speeding cab, I call up my journey: from my mountain to this river, across deserts, over rain-swept plains—alone and in good company. I've never owned less, yet carried more. It's no wonder, later, as I pull off my jeans, getting ready for bed, that denim grazes shin, and my old wound aches.

June 2008, Baderville

It's windy in Baderville. The winds blow all day, die down at night, then pick up mid-morning, intensifying in the afternoon. "Red Flag Warning," the radio announces almost every day: gusts to 45 miles per hour. The trees bend; the house creaks and pops. When I walk through the neighborhood, my hair stings my face, my body lists, my ears ache. At my feeders birds are scarce, perhaps holed up in the shelter of the woods. Once again the locals tell me, "We've never had a May or June like this. The winds always die down before May 1st. It must be you!" I wonder if I'll always be The One Who Fled From Hurricane Katrina, its curse now following in my wake, causing record snowfalls and record winds.

The temperatures are kinder, though. I've opened all my windows upstairs, curtains billowing in the breeze. It might be time at last to sleep outside. At nightfall I gather my sleeping bag, my ground pad, an extra cover and a water bottle and lug them out the bedroom door that opens onto the carport roof—that wide, flat structure I shoveled three times when the snows piled high enough to threaten its collapse. Just feet from the bedroom door, my parents have cut an opening allowing two pine trees to grow unperturbed. I put my sleeping bag outside their arc to allow an unfettered view of the sky. I lie awake, remembering a lifetime of nights like this.

In the summers, my parents piled us in the station-wagon, five children all born between 1947 and 1953. They'd haul us cross country for three straight months, from Louisville (where we lived before we moved to Tempe) to Nova Scotia, to the West coast, and the summer of 1955 all the way to Alaska with another couple, the

Furnishes, both MDs, and their brood of six. The oldest of the combined eleven was their daughter Annie, aged ten, the youngest their Gregory, still in diapers, under two. The five of us—at seven and a half, six, four, four (identical twins) and two—fell somewhere in the middle. The AlCan Highway was then unpaved. We drove across Canada and as far into Alaska as we could go—to the road's end at Fairbanks—for seventy nights sleeping out on the ground. Our sleeping bags were primitive. Somehow my parents had instilled in us a stoical grit. We'd lie awake shivering, gazing up at that awesome sky, then drift off, wake, star gaze, and fall into a final slumber just as the Dipper met the horizon, awakening to sunshine on our sleeping bags. There was no whining, no climbing into my parents' double bag to thaw ourselves out, just beauty and suffering the long summers through.

One night, somewhere in Alaska, I woke freezing cold with an aching bladder. I knew the drill: get up quietly, pee, and crawl back into the bag. But I was cold, so cold. I waited, hoping morning was near. I was six years old. Finally, unable to wait another minute or muster the courage to leave my bed, I peed in my sleeping bag. The next morning my parents scrubbed my bag, then spread it out to dry in the sun. Our travel delayed, we lingered at our campsite, my shame on display for all to see.

I'm cold now too. The wind has died, but it will take some time for my bag to harvest my body's heat. Lights still shine inside houses in the meadow, but few have turned on outside lights. We're the nation's first Dark Sky City, thanks to Lowell Observatory, where now-demoted Pluto was first sighted and named. A spotlight moon dilutes the drama of the stars overhead, but the Big Dipper still shines bright to my left, the tilted W of Cassiopeia aglow to my right. I pull the sleeping bag over my head, curl up like a lima bean, and fall asleep.

I awake two hours later to coyotes howling behind the house. After a minute, they're quiet again. The stars are now magnificent, with houses in the meadow dark, the moon having dipped behind my house. The Milky Way spreads like a mica-highway across the sky. I watch for awhile. A star falls, a bright flash overhead. Or, rather, a meteor bursts into our atmosphere, the friction causing it to burn and streak.

Last August I watched the shower of the Perseids from cushioned chairs on my neighbors' deck: Sandy, Charles, Paul and I, craning our necks to see the show. Two months ago they invited me to camp out, high on the hill behind their house. "But it was fifteen degrees this morning!" I remind them. They're undeterred, a trio who put the "hard" in "hard core." Instead, I opt to hike up with them—the only one without a pack—share their bonfire and eat the food Paul tosses on the coals when the heat allows him to venture near: sausages, potatoes, and vegetables all wrapped in foil. Sparks from the fire pop high in the air, then die before igniting the grasses growing dangerously near. At bedtime I hike back down the hill with another neighbor and her two dogs, leaving the three alone on the hill. That night, in my bed, I awaken, cold, and pull the covers back up to my neck. I think of them lying on that freezing ground, the bonfire dying to embers at dawn.

Now, in my bag, I'm warm enough to drift off again, awakening one more time in the night. It's three a. m. I can hear the train whistle down on the tracks in the heart of town, the rumble of steel wheels meeting rail. I marvel at the movement of sound over distance, the way it carries when the ground air cools below the warmer layer higher up. In August I was sleeping on this very spot at this very hour when I woke to the sound of a car down on Highway 180. In the daytime even trucks pass silently there, but now I can hear the car some two miles away. I sit up in my sleeping bag and watch the lights move along the road, then turn up Bader, coming my way. I feel fear for the first time since I moved here, into this last house back against the national forest, I alone on this high flat roof. "Don't turn, don't turn," I plead as the car approaches Suzette. It turns and drives toward Hawk Hill Road. "Don't turn," I plead again. It turns and heads up my driveway, my heart in my throat. I'd be dead and buried in a shallow grave before the police could make it out to rescue me. Then the lights disappear; the car is not on my road but Cindy's—Crow Pass—paralleling mine ten feet to the east. Nate, their boarder, is returning home from a night on the town. It's a good half hour before my heart slows enough that I can sleep again.

All these nights—inside or out—I've felt safe, though alone, as if guarded by some magical spell out of Harry Potter (*protego!*), my parents' presence so palpable here that I move in a bubble of eternal care. I ponder their legacy. My lying in this sleeping bag owes to their pioneering zeal, miles logged, nights spent camped out in open air. I remember one morning back in the sixties when, meeting my father in the kitchen, he asked, "Have you seen your mother?" "No," I answered. "Is the car there?" We looked outside to find it was. A glorious Spring had come to town, the scent of orange blossoms in the air. I knew immediately where she was. I led my father to the patio doors where, sure enough, there in her sleeping bag lay my mother, stretched out under our blossoming tree.

Now, some forty years later, I feel her blood course through my veins as we sleep outside—in memory and moment—she under orange blossoms, I under pine. Stars spin in the skies over Baderville, dance, glow, and die out in a blaze of light, all the way to dawn.

Leaving Brooklyn

It's mid-December, 2005. Snow flurries spin over Brooklyn streets as I pack up once more and say good-bye. It's over—this strange, vagabonding interlude, this hurricane hiatus of bridges and interstates, wilderness and cityscapes, solitude and fellowship. I'm going home, or what was once home. More accurately, I'm going back, to whatever back I'll find there, three and a half months after the storm. When Kate was a toddler, she would push back my bangs and, gazing at that altered face, proclaim me "not-Mom." I'm going not-home, to a not-house, in my not-town. I'm going to New Orleans.

The interstates have become old friends now. I drive them fondly, their names familiar, their loops and spurs beloved quirks. They guided me out-bound and carried me back, their beltways and clover-leafs a shaping force in my random trek, an order where there was none, a high dry path. I carry their tally—10,000 miles, every wheel rotation—in the automotive memory of my car. In my own mind I bear a less focused trace, miles mingled with music, with landscape, with memory and verse. Two registers, each accurate in its own way.

When the air becomes heavy, I know I'm close. Then the snapped trees confirm in their splintered bows that I'm following Hurricane Katrina's path. The skies are starless, as I leave Highway 59, then head west on Interstate 10, past Slidell, and over the waters to New Orleans East. It's ghost-town dark. I navigate the split, choose Canal Boulevard, and pass the Plantation Coffee House (in ruins), Delgado (a staging area), the neutral ground on Orleans Avenue (a dumping ground). Along Toulouse, the flooded cars—silt-encrusted—still line the street. Not-Home.

In the morning, I start a new life in my stricken town. My old haunts are gone—my grocery store, my gas station, my post-office, my coffeehouse. I'll have to find new ones on the dry side of the 17th Street Canal, where in its strip-mall splendor lies Metairie. Driving through its streets, I remember Bob Bourdette, a Miltonist from UNO, who died some years ago, before the storm could ravage his apartment in New Orleans East: its library—shelf after shelf of alphabetized books—its art work, its statue of Milton that Davy once called an "action figure," making everyone laugh. It was Bob who appended "deepest, darkest" to the name of this town. The addition stuck. Thereafter, whenever I crossed the line, I'd envision myself in safari gear. Now, all of New Orleans is shopping here, in deepest, darkest Metairie—at Dorignac's, Lowes, and Rite-Aid along Veterans—parking lots a nightmare, lines snaking from registers half-way down aisles.

One day at Borders, as I'm standing in just such a line, my cell phone rings. It's Janet. She's staying with a friend outside Chicago, but longing to come home. As the line inches forward, she brings me up to date. Before the storm, she had found a new apartment with no pets allowed, so had returned the favor done to her: convinced the new tenant to take on Ikey. But he left the gate open so that Ikey got out and was hit by a car. Janet helped pay the vet bill, then checked on Ikey every day to make sure he was getting his meds. Not surprisingly, on that Saturday when we both left town, it was she who rescued Ikey, taking him along in her beat-up truck with her cages of birds. But when she made it to Baton Rouge (and here the story wobbles as Janet starts to stutter) she had-had-had to have Ikey put down. She couldn't afford the v-v-v-vet bill to have the steel rod removed from his leg. Now she's unemployed, dependent on the goodwill of her old friend. "Couldn't you tutor?" I ask. "Oh, yeah," she replies.

"There's a b-b-big demand for stuttering tutors." I don't know what to say. There's no place on the roster for such casualties, for those like Janet who, still alive, won't show up in our reckonings—the official Wiki victim-count (1,836)—no rung for her, whose wound lies hidden, its pain referred from heart to tongue.

Soon after, I seek out my old Lakeview dentist, to deal with my own storm-influenced pain. Her building stands flooded in the block behind my Memphis house. In my other life I could stroll over there two minutes before my appointment time. Now I find her in Metairie, sharing a practice off West Esplanade. She looks at my tooth and shakes her head. "I've been clenching," I say, recalling those nights in Woodley Park. "You and everyone else," she replies. "Clenching and grinding. I've been making mouth guards for lots of my patients. I've made one for myself." But it's too late for me. I've cracked that tooth, providing a pathway for bacteria. She decides to fill the cavity, hoping to avoid a root canal. But two years later, my tooth still throbs. Tongue and tooth, heart and mind, and all along our city streets—under interstates—the deeper wounds: people standing on corners, talking to air.

Once more I cope by cleaning up my private world, erasing—at least outwardly—the signs of all that happened here. First I paint out the National Guard's rescue code, brown on the pink of Davy's house. Then I paint the side wall to match the front, then the faded back wall to match the side, until I've done the whole house in a popping Pepto-Bismol shade, an antidote to upset that lifts my mood. Don drives down from Baton Rouge to help me out, then tackles the problem of Davy's backyard, all leaves and limbs and chips of bark. One day he arrives with a chain-saw and loppers. While he saws the trees into foot-long logs, I bag them and carry them out to the curb. I lop off branches and bag them too. I'm finding a rhythm when, stooping by the back door steps, I tear my arm on a flood-soaked nail. Remembering Johnny's warning, I safari into Metairie where I get myself a tetanus shot. By the time I return, Don's finished an entire tree. I pitch back in. I bag for hours, then beg for a break. "Go on in," he says. "I want to finish what I've started here." But it's my job; he's only a volunteer. I've got too much pride to knock off first. When he finally flags, it's been eight straight hours of sawing and bending and lifting those logs. One week from now, Don will call me from his hospital bed, prepped for the next day's surgery: a triple by-pass. He could be dead, as my colleague Charlie Bellone will be in two short weeks, dead of a heart attack on Christmas Eve, only fifty-one; himself, perhaps, part-victim of this clean-up zeal, he, like Don, having cleared fallen trees from his North-Shore lot. But Don recovers, saving me the guilt of having let him wield that saw. Charlie's death will haunt us all, his colleagues who'd worked with him some fifteen years, who'd listened to the flute notes wafting from his cubicle—the hippie's hippie—long-haired, dream-catching, walking to his own slow tune, sashaying, sauntering—there's no word slow enough for Charlie's gait.

At Charlie's funeral students swamped the microphone —those he'd befriended, or taken in—whose tuition he'd paid, whose lives he'd changed. I sat in his backyard next to Del, listening to their stories, trying to remember when I'd seen him last. A brother recalled Charlie's own directive for today's event: "Just prop me up, a beer in one hand, a golf club in the other." He must have envisioned himself old and gray then, his slow walk slower (if that could be) his life having wound down in all good time. "Aletha," I suddenly thought, "will have to change her will." An honor student, she had told me once she was leaving her money all to him.

There will be a pall soon over the hallways of Building One, as Charlie's absence makes its presence known. It's as bad as Katrina, this fallow time, where those who survived the storm succumb to the recovery. When I next call Catherine, I pose a new word for our latest wit-game— Selecting the Scariest Hurricane Names—worse than Brownie for the B-storm, FEMA for the F-storm, Subsidence for the S-storm: *Hurricane Aftermath*, the A-storm, hands down the worst one, a season-starting killer, a head-on land-strike at Category Five.

All over New Orleans, the hurricane aftermath takes its toll. Men felling trees are felled themselves; workers on the interstate drop unsecured gear from the backs of trucks, causing fatal accidents; pot holes sink to cavernous depths; one-way signs, spun half-circle, mislead visitors, who then dodge locals who know which way the streets all run. What fails to threaten still annoys. In the Quarter, cars park on sidewalks (meter maids gone). Litter piles mount. The streets are strewn with roofing nails. Traffic creeps. Almost every intersection is a four-way stop. And I missed the hard part, was long gone, driving and hiking past the grim times here.

Before the Spring semester begins, I get a visit from my brother, Tom. He was here just weeks before Katrina, staying in my house on Memphis Street. I took him to the Quarter. Walking back, past the stores on Rampart, we noticed a sign, next to Tarot cards and voodoo dolls, which Tom then photographed and emailed to Steve: "Help Wanted (No Crack Whores Need Apply)." After the storm, every time I called him he'd always remark: "Those poor crack whores." In fact, the crack whores were better off than those of us in flooded zones—Lakeview, New Orleans East, the Ninth Ward, Gentilly—were on high ground (though no longer high) jonesing in the Quarter. I'd sent him pictures of the bathroom he'd used when he stayed with me, the tub now clogged with a tar-black grime: "Way to clean up after yourself!" Now I take him to Memphis Street to see the real thing. He snaps a picture in every room, then one of me in my living room with arms outspread as if leading a tour—the poor man's Jackie Kennedy. We go to the Ninth Ward to see what pictures can't convey: the massive scope of tilting houses, upturned cars, a church reduced to steeple and roof, all means of entry sealed beneath. If there were a hell, it would be the 9th Ward. "Through me you pass into the city of woe/Through me you pass into eternal pain...All hope abandon ye who enter here." In a fitting sequel to this dismal tour, we pass a storefront with the spray-paint sign: "Enter and be shot."

When Tom goes home, the Spring semester poised to start, I await the return of Catherine, in her new high truck, driving down from Rochester. But before she arrives, I get a call from Cynthia. She's flying down to clean up Catherine's apartment—through dust pan and Comet, to mitigate the memories there. Would I like to help? I'm ashamed at not having done this myself, used the key Catherine gave me for a cat-sitting stint, still lodged on my key chain, and done the work like some shoemaker's elf. But once again, as on that missing persons' site, Cynthia has beaten me to the draw. When we open the door on North Gayoso Street, I'm glad we are two. It's a massive job. One window is open, allowing the cats to come and go, but on every square foot of apartment floor, sit dishes that held Catherine's cat-food stash and bowls all emptied of the water she'd poured. Thereafter, the cats had an endless supply through a faucet still dripping in the bathroom sink. It's hard to imagine where to start. But Cynthia chooses the hardest task: cleaning out the bathtub where Catherine dumped all the kitty litter before she left, creating an enormous litter box, which Cynthia now tackles with plastic gloves. I start in on dishes and wash while she scoops. For hours we scrub, sweep, and carry garbage down the spiral staircase to the yard below—that dizzying structure that turns around upon itself while magically still getting somewhere. It's tricky with a bag in tow, the other hand gripping the curving rail. I remember Catherine falling here once, but even more vividly my brother Jeff's uneasiness at seeing these stairs. I email him later to pinpoint those fears. He writes back:

"I dunno. Stairs are no-man's land. They either lead to attics (cerebral otherworldliness, recesses of the brain and stuff) or to basements (underworlds, unconscious). So you're on the *umbral*. You have no figurative footing. Hitchcock would always film the staircase from an odd angle—from the ceiling in *Psycho*. All the crazy shit happens on the staircase."

No figurative footing. In any language that rings true here, the entire city on the threshold to somewhere, but caught at the moment in a limbo-spin, on those stairs that rotate—counterclockwise, like the storm itself. When Catherine was trapped here, the staircase offered no escape: below her tumult (water thigh-high), above her stasis in sweltering heat. Then the signal through the curtain, the din of blades and— magically—a savior on the top step to lead her down (all the crazy shit happens on the stairs), then up to enlightenment, freedom, escape. I wonder how Hitchcock would have filmed this scene, from below through the curving stairs to the helicopter's whirling blades—circle over spiral (turn, turn, turn)—then a flashback to the spinning winds of Hurricane Katrina, global torque pulling it toward the pole, the winds of the helicopter mimicking its dawn attack—flattening the grass —as Catherine dangles between earth and sky. When Catherine returns a week from now, she will notice what the two of us today fail to see: the mark of the helicopter's windy descent, a crop circle etched in the side-lawn's grass.

Catherine comes back after four months' absence on January 12th, 2006, in a studied link to the play *Twelfth Night*, herself like Viola, a survivor of shipwreck. She parks her high truck, climbs her staircase, and finds three cats. Naughty Guy, it seems, has been "rescued" by the SPCA, by well-intentioned volunteers, who've instead consigned him to a fate unknown. She calls to thank me for the state of her apartment and to seek out some cheer in this ailing town. We decide on the early set at d.b.a. with John Boutte, that local crooner who can melt away bluer blues than ours. But when we get there the impact is full-frontal Not-Bar. The room's the same—the parallel bars, the glowing wood, the chalkboard drink list, the smoke-encircled picture of Billie Holliday, hand lifted, singing some haunting tune. But the floor space is peopled with blank-faced strangers whose eyes meet ours with a glancing blow. The bar maids are new too; gone is that one with café-au-lait skin, crop-topped, jeans riding low on her hips. I used to imagine her cast in some local film, the essence of New Orleans exuding from her very pores, beneath the Billie Holliday photo, caught in that same haze of jazz-bar smoke.

When the band arrives, our hopes of comfort quickly fade. It's John who needs the bucking up. "I'm back," he announces into the mic, "and I'm pissed!" Then he rails against FEMA, Nagin, Blanco, and Bush. He is bellicose, profane (sing, John, sing). After ages he launches into song, giving us all what we've come to hear: "City of New Orleans,' "Treme Song," "Sisters," his heart-stopping version of Lenox's "Why." He takes an uncharacteristic break, then comes back holding a poster-sized sign, "I'M BACK. AND I'M PISSED!" The crowd laughs; we're back and pissed ourselves: at our ruined homes, our divided families, our flooded cars. His performance is deepening, not soothing our angst.

Three months from now, at the city's first Jazz Fest after the storm, he will bring down the Jazz Tent with his take on the Randy Newman song: "Louisiana 1927." He'll first sing it straight, the parallel to August painfully clear: "River rose all day; the river rose all night/Some people got lost in the flood, some people got away all right/The river has busted through clear down to Plaquemines/Six feet of water in the streets of Evangeline." Then he'll weave that link right into the rhyme: "Twelve feet of water in the streets of the Lower Nine." The refrain will become an angry claim— still believed in some hard-hit zones: "Louisiana, Louisiana. They're trying to wash us away/They're trying to wash us away." John will crank up the drama here—draw out the refrain—appealing to the audience: "Don't let 'em wash us away." "My Lord." "No, no, Don't let 'em, Don't let 'em, y'all." When he's finished, the whole crowd (on its feet) will feel his pain, will almost believe *they* blew up the levees to drive the black people out of town, then padlocked the projects to keep them at bay, the roots of racism so deep here that for a moment I believe it myself. Except that Lakeview was flooded too, white New Orleanians collapsed in attics, drowned, or exiled far from home.

When the set is over, Catherine and I heading back to her truck, we've witnessed the hallmark of this town: that swerve from the expected, performances unscripted—from set list to set length to makeup of the band itself. The word "serendipity" could have its roots here, in the dingy clubs on Frenchmen Street where the music has a life of its own, like traffic on the interstate that backs up, comes to a halt, then magically breaks up and flows unimpeded on: the rant, the sign, the laughter, then the promised tunes, a musical gumbo, always new.

One night on Frenchmen before the storm I was watching the Hot Club at d.b.a., that early performance clarinetist, Chris Kohl, would call the "Milk and Cookies Set." They've played my favorites: "Billy's Bounce," "Nachitoches Noisette," the beautiful "Azalea." Then Chris asks Mad Dog if he wants to sing. From the seat beside me, half-way in his cups, an elderly gentleman in suit and hat rises and makes his way to the stage. He sings that melancholy song that, since 9/11, is darker in tone: "I'll Never Be the Same." A hipster passing by the open door pauses, likes what he hears, and walks on in for a closer view. He turns to the barmaid and opens his arms. She reads the gesture, comes out from the bar and dances with him (stranger or friend?). Their movement becomes another instrument, adding texture to the song. As the last notes linger, he tips her backwards, they hug, then she returns to the bar as he wanders back out onto the street. When I turn back to my glass of wine, someone has filled it, perhaps in tribute to the moment just made: by band members, patron, and stranger in the night.

Impossibly, the set gets better. "John, wanna sing?" Kohl then asks. That familiar voice from a dark corner answers, "Oh, man, it's my night off!" It's John Boutte. "Just one," Kohl coaxes. "Day in the Life of a Fool." John consents and, feeding off the legacy of Mad Dog, prolongs the mood, moving with the microphone, pouring emotion into the words that, even pre-Katrina, connect with us all: "I walk the avenue/And hope I run into/The welcome sight of you coming my way. .. I stop just across from your door/But you're never home anymore." The clarinet, behind the voice, finds a place in my chest I didn't know was there. When the set is over and I walk back onto the street, I'm certain nowhere—not in New York, Chicago, Memphis or LA—has anyone bought tonight what I've heard for free, that musical lagniappe, that improvised brew.

Two summers from now, watching the dusk roll over the meadow, the bats catch insects in the air above my deck (their flight acrobatic, their leathery wings as soundless as the gathering night), of all the moments I've lived through here, it is this I will remember.

Mid-June, we're having a heat wave. It's 87 degrees in Flagstaff, but still below 40 in Baderville at dawn. My driveway is dusty, the trails more so. Coming back from a hike, I'm dirt-tinged, mid-calf to ankle. My socks are dust-coated inside my shoes. As I walk I resemble that Charles Schultz drawing of the character Pigpen, soft ground stirred up and clouding my path.

My birdbath's a magnet in this heat. I see red-shafted flickers, hairy woodpeckers, black-headed grosbeaks and flycatchers drinking in the late afternoon. Then the flash of a tanager—red on yellow—or, more beautiful still, the azure wings of the mountain bluebird perched on a fence post behind the house. Still deeper in the woods I finally see, on June twenty-first, what I've hoped for all month: three female elk with two spotted calves, born in May and still alive, despite that month's three sticking snowfalls and unrelenting howling winds.

It's 113 in the Valley of the Sun, two degrees shy of the record for this date, and ten degrees warmer than the average for June. My brother Steve and nephew Sonny come up on the shuttle to escape the heat. We decide on an overnight hike near Sedona where the waters of Oak Creek will free us from the need to carry our own, and the temperatures at night will be kinder than here. We stop at Peace Surplus, across from the shuttle stand, pick up a ground pad—self-inflating—to save my bones and four freeze-dried packets of Backpacker's Pantry.

In the morning we set out late on the West Fork of Oak Creek, half-way down the Sedona road. Steve is carrying my sleeping bag, Sonny my ground pad and back-packer's pillow. I'm traveling light by comparison, though popping

Advil less than two miles in, as my pack strains the muscles in my back and neck. Sonny, who's forgotten his shorts, is wearing (unhappily) a pair of Steve's. At seventeen he's used to the loose fit of prison-chic, shorts drooping inches below his knees. By comparison—to him—Steve's Bermuda length exposes skin. "I feel like I'm wearing a Speedo," he says. Sonny's hyperbole sets us off, Steve and I laughing our way down the path—at the vast gap between Bermuda and Speedo, the gulf between his generation and ours.

Red cliffs soar on either side of the trail we hike. Wildflowers grow out of cracks in sandstone; lichens, like petroglyphs, coil overhead. Steve calls out the names of the flowers: lupine, flea-bane, monkey flower—both red and yellow—owl clover, columbine; the names of trees: ponderosa, blackjack, sycamore, oak. If Tom or Jeff were along, we agree, they'd name the birds we hear but don't see, deep in the shade along the path. At one point we enter a stand of ferns. "Like Minnesota," Steve remarks, where we spent our summers back in the sixties, our father teaching at Lake Itasca's intensive biology summer school. Periodically, trail meets creek, with logs and stepping stones to guide us across. After awhile, we find a wide-banked site, perfect for throwing down sleeping bags. We trade our hiking boots for water shoes and wade in the creek.

The sun is brutal, the water cool. Minnows swim in the deeper pools. A water bug buries itself in the sand to escape the prodding of our sticks. Steve pumps water through a hand-held pump into plastic bags where, purified, it replenishes our drinking supply. In others he captures creek bilge to boil atop his Pepsi-can stove. It will plump up our freeze-dried hiker fare and steep the leaves of his mate drink, when the sun drops behind the cliffs so we can cook our dinner in the shade. In the meantime, we wade and talk.

94

Someone mentions poetry and, out of the blue, Sonny launches into a flawless recitation of "The Raven." I join in, having memorized it too, back in the fourth grade, its words still fresh in my aging brain. Could there be a poetry gene, I wonder, passed on along with blood type and eye shade, so that certain pairings of rhythm and rhyme will trigger an impulse to score them into cortex folds where, like petroglyphs on desert stone, they will hang preserved across the years? But why this poem and not another? This mournful exchange between poet and bird?

After dinner as the night grows cool, a wild turkey gobbles from across the creek. Sonny answers in a dead-on turkey trill: "BBBdddddddrrrrrrr." The turkey, hearing a kindred voice, replies: "BBBdddddddrrrrrrr." We all laugh. Then Sonny and turkey keep it up, this call and response across the creek, until finally he's worn it out. "Stop, Sonny," his father begs. But Sonny's seventeen. He can't stop. And it's still amusing, the interchange between boy and bird —like Poe and raven—life, as it often does, mirroring art. Attempting to end this game, Steve launches into a ghost story. Sonny listens with half an ear, the turkey quiet, until, nearing a climax, Steve intones, "And then there was a frightening sound...." Right on cue, Sonny jumps in: "BBBdddddddrrrrrrr." And this breaks us all us up, except the turkey who, unaware that his game's on hold, faithfully answers: "BBBdddddddrrrrrrr." I'm wondering how we're ever going to get to sleep, but Sonny's tired. The turkey summons twice more then, discouraged at the lack of reply, falls silent itself. The brook babbles. My pillow is soft. Before long, we're all asleep.

As always, I wake in the night. Steve's snores are masking the sound of the creek. I've slipped off my ground pad. My shoulders aching, I roll on my back to look at the sky. Instead, what catches my eye is the glow of the cliff, up-creek from our camp. It's shining as if it were late afternoon instead of midnight. There must be a full moon, though deep in the canyon, trees ringed round, I can't make it out in the light-washed sky. "If a cliff is lit up in the night," I think, "and no one is there to see the moon, is it really shining?" I can tell I'm not going to sleep much tonight, my mind turned on, my sleeping bag, over the years, having lost its loft. At four a. m. the cold rolls down the canyon walls until I'm frozen to the bone. Steve gets up and moves in closer to Sonny. For awhile, his snoring stops. Then, at five, we're both awake, drinking coffee, waiting for the sun: yesterday's enemy, this morning's friend. It's just now touching the canyon rim. Then slowly it moves down the canyon walls, then down the trees until, finally, it's warming the rocks across the creek. I realize I'm watching the inverse of what I usually see: the dusk inching up the mountain, warm becoming cool, then dark and cold.

As Sonny sleeps, Steve and I cross over to warm ourselves up. From this new, kinder vantage point we see two birds that we don't know catching flies in the air overhead. They can't be flycatchers; the head is all wrong. They're moving like bats, their colors like something out of fairy tale—"skin white as snow, lips red as blood, and hair black as ebony." We watch until they eat their full, then vanish back into the trees: two painted redstarts we will learn upon returning home, the best bird sighting I've had in years—since Wendy and I saw a painted bunting in the chigger-rich grasses outside of Dallas or Tom and I spotted a chestnut-sided warbler deep in the Minnesota woods.

When Sonny awakens, we pack up and leave this spot —now christened Turkey Camp—and head on back, Sonny in the lead, outhiking both his dad and aunt, his Speedo somewhat worse for wear. "You see," Steve points out, (though, I-Pod in ear, I'm not sure Sonny hears) "something always happens on a hike, like that turkey or those birds— or even just watching that water bug." His subtext is clear:

"Ditch those god-awful video games." But Sonny's not listening, and he's preaching to the choir when talking to me.

The sun, our morning friend, now beats down on our heads. I walk along behind my nephew, a blue bandana tied on his head, holey sneakers on his feet. He's carrying some of my gear, some of my genes, and that same poem I've toted almost fifty years—all eighteen verses—wedged in tight, underneath his bandana and the unrelenting Western sun as he heads on down the trail.

The New Normal

Now it's really over. The Spring semester has begun. Miraculously, our students have returned, enough, at least, to be taught by a pared-down faculty in four of our buildings that didn't flood. We've lost our library, our Honors Office, four classroom buildings and a slew of faculty offices. The administration building flooded too, those employees now moved to the West Bank campus across the river from our Mid-City site. It's a joyful homecoming in Liberal Arts. We hug each other by the mail boxes, asking the only question posed these days, "How'd you do?" There are only two answers: "I lost everything" or "Just some roof damage." Still bearing my own cache of odyssey-guilt, I feel for those who admit to the latter, who lower their gazes when they reply. In English alone a quarter of us have lost our homes: David, Wendy, and I (Lakeview), Paul (Gentilly), Isaac (New Orleans East), Randy (Marigny),Cathy (Mid-City), Monica (Metairie). I don't know how to classify Charlie (North Shore), who lost his life, or those like Fred who couldn't find a way to return.

Our students are older, whiter. When I take the roll in my evening class I am shocked to see I'm the only one living on the East Bank of New Orleans. There are many on the West Bank, still others from the North Shore, River Ridge, Metairie, and even La Place. They come in late, having battled traffic, driven from afar. I am careful with them, uncertain what traumas they've been through. Early on in English 062, I made the mistake of asking one, after class, if his family had evacuated for the storm. "Yes," he answered. "We all got out...except my sister. She wouldn't come. And she drowned." How many more stories there must be like this, behind the eyes staring up at me.

I'm teaching in blue jeans, unable to replace the entire wardrobe I lost in the flood. The rest of my ensemble mixes cast-offs from boxes sent by two of my sister's friends and one of my own, Han—who has since changed her name to Lily. Her box sat unnoticed in the Mid-City Post Office for weeks while she emailed me asking about it, and postal workers denied it was there. They sent another one back to its sender, getting it wrong more often than right. In the hall after class, I pass Pat, from Math, who used to show up in skirt and jacket, so together, dressed for success. Now her style mirrors mine: survivor chic. She's in blue jeans too. In May, our first graduation after the storm, we'll parade our fates in our regalia, or lack thereof, nearly half of us in street clothes, the storm having stolen our caps and gowns.

I walk to work now, down Toulouse, past the flooded cars, the litter piles, and, eight minutes later, into my office in Building One, to my working computer, my mold-free books, my postcard collection, my one surviving family snapshot, all three kids on Christmas day. Seeing these each morning when I open my door is like Christmas itself, a correction to the landscape I've passed walking here, and the one I will pass on my way to class: a head-high pile of sodden books, reeking outside the library. In a few weeks, at tables set up next to that pile, volunteers will catalogue each volume lost until, finally, the books will be gone, the smell, somewhat later, vanished too. But I'll meet it again. One day in a writing class I smell it in the classroom's air and, puzzled, scan the room. This building didn't flood. I see no mold. Everyone is quietly writing a timed in-class essay, due in an hour. When students begin to turn theirs in, the scent grows stronger. A nearing student reads my expression, points down to his pants and shoes, and sheepishly explains: "I'm gutting my grandma's house. I didn't have time to change before class." What can I say? Like all of us, he's doing the best he can, the new normal here still being defined.

On the roads I note a new preponderance of pick-up trucks, out-of-state license plates, Latino drivers. A bumper sticker has transformed too. It began with the happy claim: "New Orleans—Proud to Call it Home." Then some clever person (an English major with an ear for rhyme?) revised it to comment on the culture here: "New Orleans—Proud to Crawl Home." Now it's morphed into a post-storm joke: "New Orleans—Proud to Swim Home," a callous sticker to bear, I think, given people like my student's sister who couldn't swim, and those who drowned even though they could. By the time I leave town a year from now, it will have evolved into its schizophrenic final phase, the optimists sporting "New Orleans—*Still* Proud to Call it Home," the pessimists "New Orleans—Proud to Call it Quits." I leave my Mazda's bumper bare until I reach Arizona, where it will wear the code of its new mountain town: "FLG."

Now, as I drive through our nail-strewn streets, I listen to the CD I found in my mailbox the day I returned to work: *Hurricane Romance*, a lyrical account of life in New Orleans just after the storm by a man who stayed in his Uptown home: Phil Melancon, piano man at the Pontchartrain Hotel. A close friend of Charlie's, he's that winning combination, a performer with both wit and pipes. His gift documents those days with humor: "You've got water you can't drink?/I've got food that I can't eat./This hurricane romance is fatefully strong/Let's get together. What else could go wrong?" He sings of playing his piano in the parlor, windows open, to entertain the National Guard, of playing golf in the deserted park, of enjoying the day when the water came back on: "I showered for an hour or three/Doin' the plates, doin' my clothes, doin' the dog./

Where's that cat?" He makes even the looting seem funny, changing the lyrics to a time-worn song: "Lootin' in the morning/Lootin' in the evening/Lootin' at suppertime." There are darker moments too, a song with a grim allusion to the spray paint code our houses bear: "Death is written in fluorescent on my downtown neighbor's door." But most of the CD brings needed relief to the gruesome grind of living here. I cruise along listening, my mood enhanced by the upbeat tunes that moderate the misery I'm passing through: "You've got holes, in your shoes? I've got holes in my roof," Phil sings. "You've got mosquitoes? I've got flies. You've got gnats? I've got rats." I join in on the refrain: "This hurricane romance is fatefully strong. Let's get together. What else could go wrong?"

But most of the time, it's hard to laugh at our post-storm lives. One morning, reading my paper before going to class, I see a picture of a former student, followed by an article describing the plight of those stuck in Houston—jobless, harassed by police, living in squalor on the Southwest side. This is not the first time I've opened the paper to see students' faces staring out at me. Twice, now, I've found them in obituaries. But LeReyne is alive, though hanging by a thread: "We're all close to losing it right now," he explains in the paper's quote. "I'm not right at all," he adds, "after so long." "So long" is five months after Katrina, at which point he owns nothing but a stereo and mattress. "We don't have nothing," LeReyne explains. "Nothing. Nobody. No place to go."

It's been several years since I taught LeReyne, but I remember him well, for his winning smile, his writing skill, and the essay he wrote me, early on, describing his life in Hollygrove, that flood-prone neighborhood near the river, known for its pockets of drug-spawned crime. It's also the home of Lil Wayne, a rapper who claims in his lyrics to be "Hollygrove to the heart, Hollygrove from the start."

101

LeReyne wrote then, "I'm the last of five brothers," (or maybe it was four), but what followed remains still etched in my mind: "They were all killed. I'm my mother's last son. I'm all she's got." From then on, as I read his essays, I'd imagine his mother, heart in her throat, as she watched him set out on the mean streets of Hollygrove, crossing her fingers as he headed for Delgado, then holding her breath at night, awaiting his return.

At the end of the semester, LeReyne and his classmates filed in for their Exit Exam. He was one of the few I was sure would pass. He wrote for a full fifty minutes, turned in his bluebook, and walked out the door. The next class the students would have twenty more minutes to proofread their essays. But at that second session, there was no LeReyne. His blue book sat lonely on the edge of my desk while the other students proofread, polished, then left. Finally, I heard a commotion at the classroom door. LeReyne was maneuvering, with difficulty, into the room— on crutches, his foot in bandages, carrying with him only a pen. I felt relieved as I handed him his bluebook. He read it over, made a few corrections, and struggled to his feet to turn it in. As I walked to his desk to save him the trip, I asked, "Broken or sprained?" "Shot," LeReyne answered, flashing that grin.

Thereafter, I saw him only occasionally walking across campus. He stopped me once to tell me he had passed English 101—"on the first try," he added proudly. "I'm not surprised at all," I told him. "You can write, LeReyne." And he could.

The newspaper article now fills me in on the interlude between then and now, five months after Katrina. This promising student couldn't shake the lure of easy money on deadly streets. Although he had a job (a line cook at a popular French Quarter restaurant), he began selling drugs for extra cash, ending up in prison for a year. Then the levees broke, and LeReyne wound up in Houston. I can hear his pain in the newspaper's quotes, but also his expressiveness, his fluency:

"They say we're violent. How you expect us to act? And ain't none of us in the business of going around crying about it. But we like, damn, show us some love. But don't nobody love us. So f—them."

With pen in hand, LeReyne could transform that passage into standard prose, but here he almost raps it into print—double negatives, missing verbs—the street beat of Hollygrove in every line.

LeReyne is not the only son whom poverty and race have imperiled here, nor his mother the only parent in pain. When I first moved into my Memphis Street home, I met Aaron, who was mowing the lawn across the street. I asked him if he'd mow mine too. For years thereafter, I'd see him often, weekly in the summertime. He knew all the gossip in the neighborhood. It would be Aaron who would tell me after the storm which of my neighbors had died in the flood. He was honest, hard-working, and helpful to his kin. He was always traveling to "the country," as he put it, to help out his grandmother, other family members pitching in too. "You've got a great family," I told him one day. "I do," he answered. "They'll do anything to help you. But they won't give you nothing. You have to pay them back." (They could almost be Republicans.) But one morning he was crying as he mowed my grass. "What's wrong?" I asked. Aaron related that classic New Orleans tale. His son had been killed in a drive-by shooting a few nights before. "I did everything I could," Aaron explained. "He was hanging with a bad crowd, so I sent him out of state to live with his aunt. He was just back visiting me, and he went to hang out with his friends. He was in the wrong place, the wrong time. He was my only son." I tried to comfort him, burdened by guilt at having two sons.

A few months later, he greeted me cheerfully, asking, "Did you see the picture of my son?" He had paid for a memorial in the *Times-Picayune*. "But it hasn't been a year yet," I commented, surprised. "It's his birthday," Aaron answered. I was almost shaking as I inquired, "How old would he be?" "Eighteen," Aaron said. At that very moment, in his bed lay Davy. He would sleep until eleven; then I'd take him out for his birthday lunch. Eighteen years ago—July 31st, 1980— two baby boys were born in New Orleans, one black, one white. Now one is dead, the other sleeping, carefree in his bed. I never tell Aaron how our sons' lives crossed or, by extension, his and mine, our parenting begun that selfsame day.

LeReyne has made me think of Aaron, remember that birthday some seven years past. Now I have a brainstorm. I'll have my students write to LeReyne—a flurry of letters belying his claim, "don't nobody love us." I call the reporter who wrote the story and garner LeReyne's phone number and address. Then I give him a call, tell him I saw his picture in the paper, ask him if he'd like to get some mail. He says okay, with a smile in his voice. Then I broach the project with each of my classes. Some students are receptive; some roll their eyes. They have no use for what they see as our city's bane, that thug subculture foist happily now on some new town. I tell them LeReyne's different; he's smart, friendly, salvageable. (More eye rolls; some knowing grins.) "Just say something positive," I plead. ("Damn, show us some love.")

They write a lot of platitudes, most of them religious: "God helps those who help themselves." "God has a plan for you." "Accept Him into your life as Lord and Savior and believe." "Ask God for help, not man." But their good hearts shine through nonetheless, especially as they close:

"I believe in you." "Good luck, Your friend, Dave." "P. S. God loves you and so do I." Sometimes they offer more practical advice: "Get a Texas driver's license so they won't know you're from New Orleans." "You should probably try to clean up a little since you are trying to find a job. Maybe get a hair cut, and try wearing long sleeves and pants to cover up some of them tattoos." "Coming back to New Orleans might be your best bet. The Celebration Church on Airline has tents set up with food." "My daughter lives on the Westside of Houston, and there is an unemployment office over there off Westheimer Blvd."

Best of all, they tell him their own storm stories, of evacuating with a newborn baby, then coming home to a ransacked apartment: "They took everything I had. They even took my toothbrush." Their letters make my evacuation seem like a trip to Disneyland: "I bank with Metairie Bank. No one honored my out of state checks. The only cash I had was three dollars and twenty seven cents." Their stories remind me of that second hurricane that blew through while I was safe in DC: "I thought I was seeing the light at the other end of the tunnel. Hurricane Rita blew through Beaumont, TX . And all I could say, 'here I go again.' My five year old son and I were on the go." Not all of them, I learn, had family they could turn to: "The one thing that hurt me the most, one of my sisters that lived in Jefferson denied my son and I a place to stay. My heart was broken into two." Many describe the despair they felt when exiled from home, that same despair LeReyne speaks of here ("The end don't look too good right now"). I hope their stories will make him see that others have been where he is today and survived intact to tell their tales: "After Katrina I felt alone, down in the dumps, wondering what to do next. I sat crying many nights wondering about my family and friends." One young woman connects with this assignment, having tried once to help someone just like LeReyne:

"I hear your story, which is to me a repeat of someone else I once knew. I've been down that road before. I struggled with a man from the streets. I prayed every day for him. He was from the St. Thomas Project. He had been to jail and work on Bourbon Street as a prep cook. I helped him every chance I got. I had written up a resume, shown him another way to think, that the streets means death and it makes you angry. Everything I tried he went against. He asked me to stand by him and guide him, as his girlfriend I did my best. He cheated on me. All of my time and sacrifices went down the drain."

This must be one of the skeptics, I think, as I read her opening paragraph. I can picture her rolling her eyes as I make my case for writing to LeReyne. But she ends unjaded: "We all have seasons. Season where we cry. A season we laugh. Season of death. A season of birth, but remember enjoy every one. Life's a beauty." Dropped "s" and "ed" endings, comma splices, sentence fragments notwithstanding, I learn from the prose of the students I teach.

For the rest of the semester, every week I mail a letter or two to LeReyne. I never get a reply. He might be finding comfort in these missives; he might be laughing at them with his friends, those men he describes as "young black dudes, running around with nothing to lose": "Wait, wait, y'all, you *gotta* hear this one!" I'll never know. But one day, I see a message on my cell phone. It has a Houston area code. I retrieve it and recognize the voice of LeReyne, saying good morning to what must be his girlfriend. He's dialed my number by mistake. "I love you," he tells her (me) as he says good-bye. And that'll have to do.

***

It's been a hard semester. Everyone, students and faculty alike, has a part-time job on top of school: gutting a house, clearing limbs, holding on the phone for homeowners' agents—an experience worse than the storm itself. My flood insurance check came relatively soon, the maximum awarded for my contents and house (though I was woefully underinsured). But Farmers is subjecting me to phone-tag torture overlaid with plain old-fashioned spite. After months of calling them I finally reach an agent with a clue, who tells me my adjustor has quit, my file now languishing on someone's desk. "I am *not* going to the end of the queue," I say, with enough edge, apparently, to garner results. A few days later a new adjustor repeats the drill done months before: climbs on my roof, inspects my house, notes fences down in my backyard. Then he calls me with a quote, an amount so piddling once he's factored depreciation in that I couldn't even replace my ceilings, ruined by rain falling in through my roof. "Just send me my check," I say, so tired of it all. Mail from Farmers has come often to my post-office box: even information on contesting their awards. So every day I open my box with hope in my heart. But the check is never there. Finally I get back on the phone: "My check hasn't come, and it's been weeks," I tell the voice on the other end. "Let's see," she says, "that's 6229 Memphis Street?" "You're kidding, right?" I almost scream. "You mailed it to a flooded house? To a ghost town? That was deliberate...passive aggressive..." I'm so mad that I'm sputtering. The check has ricocheted back to Houston for resorting and redelivery, at about the same time potholes will be filled in New Orleans streets and levees built to withstand surge. She offers to cut me another check and mail it to the proper address—the one she had on file all along.

107

I rant about Farmers up and down the halls at work. But it's not just Farmers. "My homeowner's company did the same thing," says David, shaking his head. "Mailed my check to Canal Boulevard." After all we've been through, I'm shocked that these companies could be so callous. The interest accruing while those checks tour the Gulf South is plainly worth the pain inflicted. The hurricane was random, my fate the bad luck of the draw. But this act is personal. It would be easy to grow bitter here, in the aftermath of Hurricane Katrina: copper wiring stolen from homes, contractors disappearing in the night, FEMA trailers poisoning their tenants, a president gazing down unmoved from the comfort of his airplane seat. To ward off that fate, I catalogue the acts of kindness done to me: the letters and checks from family and friends; the free food at Chipotle; the care packages from Wendy's friends; the companionship of Daf on that road trip to Flagstaff; the Thanksgiving dinner at Anthea's; the clothes bought for Davy by Jim Tozzi in DC; the painting of my house from a photograph, done by Kate's friend, Christine, and given to me; not to mention the volunteers, from cities and campuses all over the country, gutting houses in the steamy day, then sleeping on floors, exhausted, at night. The balance is tipped on the side of benevolence, as Anne Frank taught us sixty years ago: "In spite of everything I still believe that people are basically good at heart."

These good-hearted people show up on weekends in New Orleans streets, having learned the cavalry's *not* on the way. They unload their lawnmowers from the backs of trucks and mow the grass in City Park. They hang hand-made street signs to replace the ones the storm blew down. They clean up swaths of city streets, with the newly-formed Katrina Krewe, who've gathered up rakes, trowels, brooms and garbage bags, then mobilized citizens on Wednesdays and Saturdays to bring back the charm of this hard-knock town. Catherine and I join in one Saturday, for three hours cleaning up Esplanade from the river north to Rampart Street. We feel happily exhausted when we get through. But three weeks later, driving down to d.b.a., it's hard to look out the windows of the car, the street right back to the way it was.

It's about time, I realize, to tend to my own patch of storm-blown land. My house remains as Katrina left it, down to my refrigerator, still lying on its back, blocking access to the hall. This EPA-cited hazardous container should be sitting on my curb, waiting for the white-goods truck to haul it to the dump where Latino workers will drain its Freon and muck it out. I call up Danny, a neighbor, and ask for his help. He's got a truck and a wiry frame. He'll be by on Saturday to pick me up. When he arrives, he's brought a companion, the daughter of his girlfriend, nine-year-old Blaine. We head for Delgado to pick up a dolly. "There's my school," Blaine says, as we pass by a building standing ruined in the morning sun. She's had a hard time in the last few months, the loss of her school the least of her woes. She wound up at the Convention Center after the storm, no one having had the sense to evacuate with her and keep her safe. It's hard to imagine the things she's seen in her nine-year span. But she's cheerful today, on an outing with her almost-Dad. When we make it to Memphis Street, she registers no shock at the state of my house. But Danny scans the kitchen and says, "On your deathbed, you'll remember this." I have no way of knowing if this is true, but I do know his prophecy will haunt me for years.

We get the refrigerator on its feet without too much trouble, tape it closed, and use the dolly to push it toward the door. But there we're in trouble. The opening's too narrow. "Do you have a hammer?" Danny asks. I remember the weights that I walked with through the neighborhood in happier times, find them in the living room, and hand one to him. He bashes in the refrigerator's handles, gaining another two inches of room. But the bulky appliance still won't fit, and Danny's getting frustrated. He rips off the screen door and hurls it into my backyard. Then he rips off the door frame, sends it flying too. Now we're getting somewhere. He positions himself outside and pulls while I push from inside, trying to get some traction on the dirt-caked floor. Then Blaine, who's been wandering in the yard, gets a little too close as Danny pulls. "Blaine!" he yells, spewing a string of profanities that shock even me. But Blaine's unfazed, clearly used to language like this. At least, I reason, he's worried about her well-being. However he may do it, he's one adult who'll keep her safe.

We're almost there now, Blaine wandering by the backyard fence, the refrigerator half-way through the door. But suddenly a mucousy liquid starts to seep from the freezer compartment onto the floor. I lose all my traction as the liquid pools beneath my feet. "Push!" Danny yells. "One good push." Oh, this is rich, I think, as the liquid— slick as amniotic fluid—continues to leak and Danny to holler, "Push! Push!" In the end it's Danny's pulling, not my pushing, that gets results, the refrigerator popping out onto the porch. Now we just need to walk it down the three porch steps, then push it out onto the curb. But the wheels of the dolly have since collapsed. "Stand back!" Danny cautions, mustering his strength to ease it down himself. But human will is no match for weight combined with gravity: the refrigerator crashes down the steps, its door popping open as, from deep within, there emerges a scent on my deathbed I'll recall: old flower water, bad shrimp, toe jam, rotten eggs, silent farts—greed, vanity, slander, and envy—all combined into an uber-scent that fills the air. And here we lose all our resolve. I'll come back later, we decide, with duct tape for that open door; then Danny will follow to haul it to the curb.

Back at Davy's I invite both Danny and Blaine inside. She bangs on the piano. I give her a coke. As she leaves, I say, "Thank-you, Blaine, for all your help." This is silly, we both know. She didn't help at all. But she's a child in need of a few kind words. "You're welcome," she replies.

The semester drags on. I mail my letters to LeReyne, teach my classes, read my paper. For the most part, the newspaper stories are grim. But one day the front page goes over the top, reporting the murders of four New Orleanians —execution style, drug related—in a Slidell trailer park some thirty miles away. Two others survived. "Mother, daughter hid during slaughter," the headline says, beneath it adding: "They crouched in bath as four gunned down." It's that age-old story, I think as I read: the seventh kid, evading the wolf, by hiding in the grandfather clock; the ninth nurse, foiling Richard Speck, by hiding underneath the bed. "Can't these murderers count?" I wonder as I read. A neighbor describes the daughter "crying hysterically, her hair still full of conditioner from the bath." I skim through the rest of the article, time running out before my nine o'clock class. When I get to work, my colleagues have read this story too; we share our shock as we run to class. When I return, I see another colleague, with the same gruesome topic on her lips. "Did you read about those murders in the trailer?" she asks. "Boy, did I," I answer. "Wasn't that awful?" "You know who the girl was," she says in a lowered voice. "It was Blaine."

When I get home from work, I reread the article, every word now taking on a meaning that I missed before, the horror intensified by knowing it was Blaine. It is she, just nine, whose eye-witness account is quoted there: "One of the intruders declared, 'Now you motherf—s are going to die!', and the shooting started *the girl* told a neighbor." It

111

was she, waiting in the bathtub in "excruciating" silence, then "emerging to find four family members dead on the living room floor." It was she who must have watched as her mother took a cell phone from one victim's pocket to call for help. It was she to whom a neighbor refers in the heart-felt quote:

"This poor little kid has been through absolute hell," Conley said. "She's seen things that I wouldn't wish on my worst enemy, things that no 9-year-old should ever have to see."

Blaine's, like LeReyne's, is a story whose ending I will never know. She may develop a stutter, a fear of the dark, an inability to concentrate, or she may move beyond this, the memory faded as she reaps the joys of children, career, and a long-term mate until, at last, she but dimly remembers the crouching silence, the threat, and then the follow through, the desperate search for the cell phone, the call for help, and then finally, at the very end, on her death bed, the images resurfacing—she'll remember this.

It's monsoon season in Flagstaff. Lightning flashes over the peaks. Thunder claps. Then the rain beats down, soaking the cinders and sending up the scent of pine. I check the forecast before dragging my sleeping bag outside at night or walking up onto Rudd Tank Road in the afternoon, miles from the shelter of my house.

A cool breeze blows through the north-face windows over my deck. Birds take shelter in the woods. A chipmunk returns to the woodpile under my carport where it seems to live. I wonder where the elk are waiting out this latest storm, whether the calves still have their spots.

A week ago I had the rarest sighting, one that I may never witness again. At five a.m. a heart-stopping bugle right under my window jolted me awake. I looked outside and saw three female elk, one youngish calf and two spotted babies, the same ones I'd seen just weeks before. But this time they were grazing in the shadow of my house, one baby resting in the grass. As I watched, it got to its feet and bounded over to its mother to nurse. At last count, I'm one of few neighbors who has seen a nursing elk, I, the newest addition to Baderville, barely free of spots myself.

In moving here I've entered an animal paradise: coyotes singing in the night, jackrabbits hiding in the tall grass beside my deck, hawks soaring overhead, a kaleidoscope of birds competing with the Abert's squirrels at the feeders in my trees. One squirrel keeps me on my toes all day, raiding my feeder—knocking it down—seed scattered on the ground. I pelt him with pinecones; he's undeterred. Finally, I buy him his own supply of squirrel food and place it on a picnic table far from the house. He eats his fill, then comes to my feeder for dessert, knocking it down yet again. In the grand scheme, I know I'm more intelligent than he, but he's besting me here, possessed of a deep cache of forest-smarts I've yet to acquire.

At least I've mastered mouse control. Bob, of the Hart Prairie fire, has put me onto a new, better mousetrap. The mouse, lured by peanut butter, triggers a switch that releases the voltage of four AA batteries then, zapped, dies quietly within its walls: no more sprung traps with bait consumed or, worse, maimed mice, suffering as hammer catches limb instead of neck. In the dead of last winter, I had set a trap in the sunroom the night before. I got up in the morning to see that I had caught a mouse. But when I picked up the trap, the mouse began wiggling as I saw the hammer had failed to kill it, only crushed one of its limbs. I burst out onto the back deck, where Frank, my visiting friend, was balanced precariously on a chair, broom in hand, knocking the snow off the TV dish. "My God!" I yelled, releasing the mouse right onto the snow and watching it limp away to die a death only slightly worse than the night it had just suffered through. "That's it," I vowed, Frank as my witness. "I'm never setting another trap."

That wounded mouse set free a memory of animal misery I'd caused years before. One Sunday in my senior year at Colby College, high on a hill in the wilds of Maine, I was having trouble writing a paper. I had wandered out into the hall and was gazing through the glass, waiting for words. A gust of wind blew up in my face from the hopper window tilted in at my feet. Without lowering my gaze, I used my knees to push it closed, a process that set off a high-pitched "eeeee," then another and another as doors flew open and my dorm mates convened to see what was wrong. A bat had been hanging underneath the window; when I closed it, the metal corner had bitten into the animal's neck. Mortally wounded, it was sending out a series of bat-shrieks. I looked down into that near-human face, blood oozing out, and turned away. I should have just opened, then closed the window again, severing its head and putting it out of its misery. Instead, I waited. Someone suggested calling B and G (Buildings and Grounds), but before we managed to make the call, the shrieking stopped, the bat having died and dropped four stories to the snow below.

No one finished her paper that day. We gathered in my room and talked. I can still remember Sue, from Bangor, pinning on me a "crime against the animal kingdom," and my roommate, Terry, floored by a coincidence: she was writing a paper on a single passage from Joyce's *Ulysses*, one, in that massive tome, that mentioned bats.

I was thinking of something else, of years ago in Louisville when, just a child, I was playing in the front yard near our quiet street, Eagle Pass Road. From out of nowhere, a car came speeding down the street. As it passed just in front of me, someone threw a kitten out the open window. It landed in the street before me—one eye hanging from its socket—and let out a feeble cry that became in a second a gurgle, as blood welled up inside its throat. In a flash, my mother appeared with a rock, fell to her knees in the street, and bashed in the kitten's head. I remember feeling a wave of relief, my mother having acted instinctively, without a thought having done the right thing. Clearly, the courage-gene has passed me by, the dither-gene acquired instead, my nature—contemplative—making me hesitant, slow to act.

From my window now, almost forty years since the crime against that bat, I watch the clouds building over the peaks, threatening rain, and think of the animals left in New Orleans three summers ago, as another storm loomed—even now, their suffering too painful to contemplate long. There's something about that inarticulate animal state that

115

tears at the heart, especially at the thought of dogs, drawn to the pack, but left behind. There ought to be some tribute paid them, I think, along the lines of the coffee house across from Macy's, dedicated to the late dog, Biff. At Biff's Bagels and Internet Cafe, walls and counters—every spare inch of space—are covered by photos of deceased pets, carefully framed, their names, dates, and owners' messages stenciled in. It *was* Biff's that I first discovered when I came to Flagstaff, after that cross-country drive with Daf. I would buy my bagel and use the computer with the dogs of Flagstaff gathered round. There were (and still are) my favorites: "My Best Buddy, Sunny Pup"; "Taffy, The Original Party Animal. He Was Once Tasted by a Coyote"; "Gus, Rafting on the Verde"; "Lizzy, She Never Let Blindness Get in the Way of Fun." One woman finds the pictures not quite enough, attaching a narrative to "Lesotho's Maximillian, 1967-1976." I sit down one day and read it. Her father, a biology professor, just like mine, moved the family to South Africa during the Vietnam War. There, they found Maximillian in a pet store and, through him, were "healed of loneliness for the Sonoran desert." They returned to the states because of apartheid, leaving the dog with a friend until he was shipped back to them: "The international airport resounded with yelps of joy upon his arrival." Her story ends: "He was like a brother to us, and when he died out in the desert, his spirit came to say goodbye."

This café is a canine version of National Public Radio's Story Corps, a massive photographic essay, capturing the vibe of this dog-friendly town. I have one surviving picture of Eightball, water-damaged, but her image clear: sitting on the couch in the living room. She needs to be here, I decide, with these Flagstaff mascots and Tom's dog Noodles, "1989-2005: Forever in My Heart." I buy a frame, a sharpie, and (thinking of those unmarked graves in the cemetery by the trailer park), in my best hand write: "Eightball ('Eightie'): October 1989-May 2002. Buried in New Orleans, Remembered Here." A counter worker puts her by the register for patrons of the store to see when picking up their bagels, counting out their change. I understand now Aaron's grin, as his son's memorial hit the newsstand, thousands of people seeing it and maybe reading the words he wrote. I can't help smiling myself as I buy my bagel, say a mental "good morning" to Eightie, then go across the street to Macy's where it's quiet and easier to work.

So much remembering: dogs and people and houses and trees, the city of New Orleans—as it was, as it's become. The rain over Baderville turns to hail, pelting the petunias on my deck, while on the peaks, even now, mid-July, it swirls as it did mid-December, turning to snow.

Razing a House

The semester's over—Spring 2006—only one more year until I retire and move west to my Hawk Hill home. In the meantime I have a job on top of summer school: finding renters for Davy's house, whose mortgage payment, thanks to hiked insurance rates, now totals $1350 a month and is bleeding me dry. Then I can move into trailer 30 and bulldoze my house, so I can leave unfettered, walk boldly away. At least twice a week now, after work, I've been driving by it, going inside, and seeking out that one last item which, if only recovered, will cancel out the loss accrued, will somehow restore my balance, that gem lying just beneath the surface under upturned dresser or mold-caked book. But I never find it, each time departing empty-handed with the memory of how, empty-handed, I left before. This has got to stop, I tell myself; this house has to go. It's becoming an obsession, an unhealthy pastime whose only cure lies in all-out severance from the rafters and bricks still standing here. I call up Fidelity and make plans to bulldoze my Lakeview home. But it's not that simple. To qualify for funds to either bulldoze or raise the house, I must document its status as "substantially damaged." That's easy, I think; I've found this proof on the internet, my house both in a flood zone and more than 50 percent destroyed. But that's not good enough, they say. I must go down to City Hall with pictures of my damaged house and bring back official forms confirming this is so.

I set out early on a Friday, our summer school scheduled on a four-day week. Parking is a challenge; finally I opt to walk several blocks to that honey-combed structure on Perdido Street. The line in the building snakes down the hall, everyone carrying their pictures, looking haggard, inching forward until finally we make it to the office door and then, inside, move onto chairs. There won't be a house left standing in New Orleans, I think, looking back at the growing line and then ahead to the city workers, leafing through pictures, filling out forms. But when those of us sitting start to talk, I learn few are here to confirm their loss. Instead, they're contesting that designation—"substantially damaged"—and seeking permission to build back just as before. On my very block, I will see in time only one house raised (my neighbor's to the north), only two houses bulldozed (mine and one across the street), the rest restored to their pre-flood form. Clearly, it doesn't take much to convince the official of whichever option we desire. One by one we leave with a smile, three photos left behind for the city's files, one official paper in hand.

My document secured, I fax it to my flood insurer, choose a demolition company, get my estimates, notarize forms, fax them, make more phone calls, wait. It seems like forever until finally I'm assigned a date. But there's still one more hurdle I'll have to clear, number seven on Colonial Claims' requirement list: "Photograph the work in the beginning and in progress along with the end result." "In progress?" This can't be right, I think, calling up Colonial to hear, I assume, "Oh, no, of course not; just photograph your house and then the empty lot once it's been razed." Instead, the agent tells me I must indeed take pictures of my house as it's being destroyed. Otherwise, she explains, I could have photographed just any lot, pocketing the money for myself. "But why couldn't I take a "before" shot, including part of the house next door, then an "after" shot: my vacant lot with that same house in view?" Somehow that won't do. I'll have to not only watch, but photograph the walls of my house as they tumble down.

I'm dreading this day, imagining myself, camera in hand, watching—in addition to my house collapsing—my

119

personal possessions taking wing, underwear from dresser drawers winding up on my neighbor's tree. I'm not alone in this anxiety. "Underwear?" a Lakeview friend replies when I tell him my fears. "You're worried about underwear? How about my house? Gay porn floating through the air." We both laugh, our worries seeming silly once uncovered and shared. But there's one real concern: the grave of Eightball, just below the kitchen porch, underneath the spot where my screen door, tossed by Danny, came to rest. Davy hadn't dug the hole that deep when I placed her there, wrapped in a yellow towel, then swore off pets forever, almost two years ago. I'm afraid of seeing her bones resurface as the bulldozer rips out the sweet olive tree: the yellow towel flash, the skeleton—caught in a snare of roots—rise, then tumble and break apart. But there's no solution to this deepest fear, short of digging her up and reburying her myself in some shady corner of Davy's backyard. But I don't have the courage; I'll just have to hope she's lying deep, and will lie there—forever placid—out of range of the bulldozer's teeth.

The day arrives. Kate is home from Oberlin, asleep. I wonder if I should wake her up or let her sleep unruffled, she and Eightball (I'm hoping) missing it all. But this might be, I reason, like missing a funeral, left without closure, then cloying guilt. I wake her up, and we set out for Lakeview, three men and a bulldozer parked in my yard. We talk for awhile. Then one removes my brass address and hands it to me. He doesn't suggest, as another man did to my colleague, Randy, that I throw a brick through my window, as I've "always wanted to," just for fun. I could never have done that, as Randy did, my feelings for my house still tender, even as I've commissioned its death. On a losers' continuum, I lie midway between the rock-throwing Randy, and Alice, who teaches ESL. In gutting her house, she hand-wrapped each possession, then placed it gently in the trash.

Now, as I place my address plaque on the ground and grip my camera, the bulldozer rumbles to life, its first bite tearing into my roof. This is going to be fast, I see, as a huge chunk of shingles and tar paper falls, exposing the rafters. Another bite lays bare the mold strip lining my living room wall, then the green of the bedroom belonging to Kate. "Oh!" she says. I painted her room while she was away her sophomore year, a cool grey-green, setting off the white of bookshelves and comforter atop her bed. I snap a picture as the bulldozer climbs high onto the debris pile, then another as it breaks off a mammoth chunk, exposing the blue of my bathroom tiles. "They're so beautiful," I say to Kate. I always loved that sky blue sheen behind the arc of the shower and tub. I hung a white eyelet shower curtain over the white ceramic floor, then stenciled a black vine where blue tiles met white walls, the combination cool and clean. The tiles are suddenly gone now too, the bulldozer climbing high, king of the mountain, my house a rubble heap underneath. Snap. Snap. My underwear worries were all unfounded; nothing emerges from beneath the weight of those boards and bricks—and water, two men hosing the pile to keep asbestos dust at bay. "Had enough?" I ask Kate. She has. We leave before the bulldozer tackles the tree. That's another ending I'll never know: whether Eightie was exhumed, then tossed in the dumpster, or whether she's resting still, undisturbed in my empty lot. Either way, Kate and I will have driven off, will have left our thirteen-year pet behind.

The next day I drive down Memphis Street and stop my car where a house once stood. My lot is empty, the dirt still bearing the caterpillar's tread. I walk through the space, from the sidewalk to the alley fence. At about mid-yard I find, peeking through clods, some small blue chips of bathroom tile. I pick up five and carry them away, cerulean wedges aglow in my hand, like little pieces of the sky.

The semester over, my house now gone, Catherine will soon be leaving too. She's found a job in North Carolina, at UNC Greensboro, a place she will come to label "white bread," after living for eight years in this town. For the summer she'll be a visiting scholar at the Folger Library in DC. By chance, Chris is going to a conference in London. He'll be gone two weeks. "Do you want to use my apartment?" he asks. I jump at the chance, and fly off to the Capital, where I spent those weeks as an evacuee.

It's been less than a year since I wandered here, sometimes joyful, sometimes bereft. I can still remember the almost-panic of being homeless, the hours I walked the steamy streets—courting exhaustion—the sound of the gibbons across the trees, the Monk competition, the protest march. I walk by the house in Woodley Park, but don't go in, Elena having since moved on, taken a job in San Francisco. I didn't know her roommates all that well. Stopping at the corner, I buy a copy of the Washington Post and walk to Tryst, over Ellington Bridge, dodging joggers, looking into the wide expanse of Rock Creek Park.

I'm calmer now, my future taking semi-shape. I've put a For Sale sign in my lot—for the second time—someone having stolen the first. I suspect my neighbor, who calls me with plans to buy my land, then flakes, makes another offer, then flakes again. He's afraid of who might buy it instead and build so close—a huge McMansion that will steal his privacy and block his light. Two years from now my hunch will be confirmed when someone steals the sign of the realtor I hired when I moved away. A neighbor across the street will tell me, "I saw it in Mr. Joe's backyard, propped

123

against his house," my realtor now out fifty bucks. But it won't be my problem anymore.

I ride the subway to visit Catherine, time no longer heavy on my hands, my nights— unbroken— made for sleep. We go to a Farmer's Market, have a meal in a sidewalk café. She shows me the Folger with its separate entrances, one for scholars and one for the hoi-polloi, winners and losers, I think, again.

While she's working, I walk up Connecticut and visit the zoo. It's all mothers and children, strollers bottlenecking every path. I watch the animals and listen to the families, the mothers like teachers, this summer day a field trip with, probably, a recap at dinnertime with Dad. It's impossible to tally the head start these children have, their mothers not working—so focused and relaxed—devoting the summertime to their kids. It's hard not to think of New Orleans' children—what they've been through, how they lag behind—as the lessons unfold, biology and manners, the way being paved for acceptance into Sidwell Friends, then Yale or Swarthmore down the road: "The cheetah is a mammal, just like us. You see its hair? And it feeds its babies milk. Stand back, now, and let the young lady have a look." At one exhibit a little girl, probably four, leans over the moat with her mother's camera. The mother snatches it, avoiding a sure catastrophe. But the child throws a tantrum: "You grabbed it!" she screams, over and over. "And it's not nice to grab!" I can't wait to see how the mom handles this. "You're right," she says. "I shouldn't have grabbed it. I should have asked you nicely to give it to me. But I was so afraid you'd drop it, and then, just think. We couldn't show our pictures to Daddy. Now, wouldn't that be sad?" She's a genius, I think, the child immediately calming down. Fathers, I see, loom large in this world.

Now I've come to the pandas, my goal all along. The baby panda, too young for viewing when I last was here, now romps with its mother as a huge crowd forms. I can measure in the panda's growth the time elapsed between then and now, the distance we've come. The little cub is delighting the crowd. It lumbers under a clump of brush. "It's making a fort!" a little boy yells. The children all relate, having made forts themselves. When the cub emerges, it heads for a tree and starts to climb, paw over paw, swaying, clearly a novice at this panda skill. His huge mother shuffles over and climbs up after him—to keep him safe, we all assume. But she's swinging her leg right at his head. Is she trying to connect? It looks like she is. Her leg strikes his torso, causing him to lose his grip. We gasp. But he hangs on, climbs higher still, with the mother in pursuit. This time she knocks him loose; he tumbles to the ground as the crowd holds its breath. Is this panda tough-love, I wonder? The quickest way to teach a cub to hold on tight? But the cub's okay. Undeterred, it gets up and heads right back to the tree.

If this were a novel, that cub would be a symbol, but here it's just a bear. It climbs back bravely, limb by limb— just a little worse for wear—swaying, slipping back (collective gasp!) and then recovering, moving—one paw at a time—over branches in the morning sun, all the way to the top.

Afterword

Catherine is back teaching at UNO, living in the same apartment she was rescued from, and caring for her two remaining cats, Lily and Elsie. Mikey, the third survivor, disappeared when she was in Greensboro. When Hurricane Gustav threatened in 2008, both cats and mistress fled to Jackson.

Don rode out Hurricane Gustav in the house that harbored me during Katrina. The tree whose branch barely missed my car then, came down this time, along with one other, piercing the roof and ceiling of his house. Don was unhurt.

Del hosted no one during that same storm; no overflow filled up the hooker motel.

Janet, who now lives in southern Illinois, returned to New Orleans for the first time in May 2010. She and Del went to Jazz Fest. Her stutter, though improved, still makes employment difficult.

Daf still lives in Payson, Arizona, awaiting a future real estate boom.

Cynthia stays in touch with Catherine and visits every Jazz Fest.

Chris has moved from DC to LA to Princeton to Cambridge and now, 2010, is back in DC. His second book, *Storm World: Hurricanes, Politics, and the Battle Over Global Warming*, owes much to Hurricane Katrina. Its first chapter, "6229 Memphis Street," describes my storm-ruined house.

Just after I left New Orleans, Davy, Angela, and Linda returned, Davy having won a two-year stint with the Thelonious Monk Institution's seven-person jazz band. The institute had just relocated from Los Angeles to New Orleans to promote jazz education there. The three have now resettled in Astoria.

Kate graduated from Oberlin in 2008, returned to New Orleans, and, with three roommates, moved into Davy's house on Toulouse. I gave her my Mazda as a graduation present.

The Hot Club of New Orleans and John Boutte still play on Frenchmen Street. The Pontchartrain Hotel has been converted into luxury apartments for seniors. Phil Melancon now plays at Le Pavillon.

The trailer park on Delgado's campus has been removed. When I visited the graveyard in January, 2009, there were no quarters on the Buddy Bolden memorial, just an empty single-serving liquor bottle.

The homeless camp under the interstate at Claiborne Avenue is gone. Brad Pitt's contemporary, green-built houses rise out of vacant lots in the Lower Ninth Ward, near where the levee broke.

In May, 2008, I sold my lot on Memphis Street to my neighbors across the street and four months later bought a house in Tucson. When I visited Memphis Street in 2009, they had yet to build on it. Mr. Joe's house next door (a foreclosure) had a For Sale sign out front. At that point, no one had stolen it.

In April 2010, after record snowfalls in Baderville, the carport roof where I used to sleep collapsed in the late afternoon. I had been gone for over a year by then, but my neighbors Mike and Karen heard the boom as they were walking along Suzette Lane. Not until the next day did they make the link to a fresh pile of rubble up on Hawk Hill Road.

At nearly five years old, Tai Shan, the National Zoo's panda, returned "home" to China. Once more, our paths converge.

Eightball may or may not be buried in my lot.
Blaine and LeReyne may or may not be okay.
New Orleans will be okay.
Charlie will be remembered.

Sources

Lee, Trymaine. "Haven and Hell. Future Looks Grim for Some Left to Fend for Themselves." *Times-Picayune.* 12 Feb. 2006.

Rioux, Paul. "Mother, Daughter Hid During Slaughter: They Crouched in Bath As Four Gunned Down." *Times-Picayune.* 27 Jun. 2006.

Made in the USA
Lexington, KY
29 June 2011